THE
HUNGRY
Camper
COOKBOOK

MORE THAN **200** DELICIOUS RECIPES TO COOK AND EAT OUTDOORS

spruce

An Hachette UK Company
www.hachette.co.uk

First published in Great Britain in 2015 by
Spruce, a division of Octopus Publishing Group Ltd
Endeavour House
189 Shaftesbury Avenue
London
WC2H 8JY
www.octopusbooks.co.uk

ISBN 978-1-84601-482-6

A CIP catalogue record for this book is available
from the British Library

Printed and bound in China

10 9 8 7 6 5 4 3 2 1

Cooking times given for the recipes in this book
should be used as a guide only – always check food
is cooked through and piping hot before eating. The
juices of poultry should run clear when the thickest
part is pierced with a sharp knife.

Contents

Introduction

No one can forget the excitement of their first camping holiday. The passing of years tends to add a romantic slant to the whole experience, with campfires, toasted marshmallows and nature walks helping to erase memories of soggy sleeping bags, torrential rain and numb toes. There's no denying the thrill of a camping trip – from the planning and packing, to choosing a pitch, setting up camp and cooking food over an open fire.

Camping provides a rare chance to connect with your inner child, reigniting the adventurous spirit that has been worn down by the daily grind. And kids thrive on the freedom and adventure of a holiday where the regular routine is tossed aside and no one nags them about personal hygiene. It's also a great opportunity to give them some responsibility, which will be richly rewarded by the freedom they'll enjoy.

If you're going to fully embrace the camping experience, it's best to leave the modern world at home as far as possible. It's difficult to bond with nature if you're trying to get a Wi-Fi connection to pick up work emails, or you cut short the campfire banter to go inside and watch telly. Camping is all about removing yourself from the frenetic pace of everyday life and taking a step back to basics. It's about having a conversation over dinner, rather than sitting in silence on the sofa; it's about teaching your kids that nature can compete with smartphones and tablets on the entertainment front. And of course, it wouldn't be a true camping experience without spending at least one entire day inside watching the rain pour down.

WHAT TO PACK

When you pack for a camping trip every scrap of space is at a premium, which is why you need to be methodical – perhaps verging on the obsessive – about making lists and getting organized well in advance of departure day. Unless you have all your camping kit and supplies constantly packed up and ready to go at a moment's notice, you'll need to begin preparations a week or so beforehand. The last thing you want to do on holiday is spend hours trekking around out-of-town shopping centres searching for vital bits of equipment that you forgot to pack.

The exact contents of your car will be dictated by the type of camping 'camp' you fall into: purists will take the bare minimum and will be happy to survive on canned food and one change of clothes; glampers will need a few more luxury items in order to enjoy the experience; and those travelling with kids will be lucky to get away with an inch of free space remaining in the car or van.

TENT

If you're camping under canvas, your tent and sleeping kit are obviously the big priorities and will also take up the most amount of space. As a rough rule of thumb, the bigger the tent the more likelihood there is of everyone still being on talking terms by the end of the holiday. If you can afford to, buy a tent with separate sleeping and living areas and enough space to stand up straight and move around – it might not seem such a big deal during a heat wave but you'll appreciate the extra space when that freak thunderstorm unleashes itself over the site.

BEDDING

If you love the idea of camping but also love the idea of getting some sleep while you're on holiday, it's definitely worth considering inflatable mattresses or air beds. Sleeping mats have their place but it's usually on survival expeditions. There's no shame in packing a few home comforts and your joints will thank you for it in the morning. If you have space, bring duvets and pillows as well: it gets cold in a tent at night. If you think about it logically, the only thing separating you from the elements is a sliver of man-made fibre – why on earth wouldn't you bring a few extra sleeping layers? You'll have the last laugh when the temperature plummets and you're snuggled up in your 15-tog double duck-down duvet.

LIVING & SLEEPING CHECKLIST

- ☐ Tent, tent pegs and mallet
- ☐ Groundsheets
- ☐ Sleeping bags
- ☐ Duvets and pillows
- ☐ Air bed and pump or sleeping mats
- ☐ Fold-up table and chairs
- ☐ Rugs and blankets (for chilly evenings)
- ☐ Towels
- ☐ Wet weather gear
- ☐ Spare socks
- ☐ Flip flops (for shower and toilet trips)
- ☐ Wellies and hiking boots

FIRST AID

You can pretty much guarantee that someone will get a cut, bite, headache or stubbed toe within minutes of your arrival so a well-stocked first aid kit is essential. If you've used it before, always check it before you pack and top up anything that has run low. Keep the kit somewhere easy to access and make sure everyone knows where it is so there's no fumbling around for sting relief in the middle of the night.

KEEPING CLEAN

The camper's code accepts that grooming standards can be lowered – queuing for a shower that wouldn't be out of place in a penal colony is a sure-fire way for personal hygiene to take a nose dive. It's a bit like eating garlic: if everyone becomes a soap dodger, no one will notice the smell. But, there should be a token nod towards grooming and you should at least pack towels, shower gel, shampoo and toothpaste. And it goes without saying that you can never have enough toilet paper.

FIRST AID & TOILETRIES CHECKLIST

- [ ] Toothbrushes and toothpaste
- [ ] Razor and shaving cream
- [ ] Shower gel
- [ ] Shampoo
- [ ] Deodorant
- [ ] Toilet paper
- [ ] Hairbrush and hairbands
- [ ] Nail scissors and tweezers
- [ ] Sun cream
- [ ] Insect repellent
- [ ] Antihistamine
- [ ] Thermometer
- [ ] Antiseptic cream
- [ ] Plasters and bandages
- [ ] Painkillers
- [ ] Prescription medication

OTHER USEFUL EQUIPMENT

- [ ] Camera
- [ ] Mobile phone charger
- [ ] Clock radio
- [ ] Travel clothesline and pegs
- [ ] Multi-tool and penknife
- [ ] Torch
- [ ] Maps and compass
- [ ] Sewing kit
- [ ] String
- [ ] Travel wash
- [ ] Umbrella
- [ ] Duct tape
- [ ] Wet wipes
- [ ] Ear plugs (for next-door snorers!)
- [ ] Coins (for showers or lockers)
- [ ] Toys and games

COOKING EQUIPMENT

The amount of equipment you bring depends on whether you intend mealtimes to be a central focus or just a chance to refuel. You will need a decent double-burner camping stove at the very least, with plenty of spare fuel to see you through the trip. If you're planning on embracing the romance of alfresco dining and cooking on a campfire, you should bring fuel (wood or barbecue coals). It's worth checking in advance if the campsite allows open fires and sells fuel, as this could be something less to carry.

A lot of camping recipes are designed for cooking in one pot so make sure you bring one large enough for the whole party. A frying pan is also essential for morning fry-ups. Bring enough dishes and cutlery for everyone to eat together without playing 'pass the fork', and don't forget wine glasses – unless you want to tip the coffee dregs out of a mug when evening approaches.

COOL BOXES

If you don't have a camping fridge, you will need to take at least one cool box with you. As a rule ground meat, poultry and fish shouldn't be kept for more than two days but steaks and chops will keep for three to four, and eggs, cured bacon and other dairy products should keep in sealed containers for up to a week. Some campsites have freezers available so you can re-freeze your ice packs, so mark them with your name.

When packing your cool box, use every bit of space, fill any gaps with bubble wrap and try not to open it too often. If possible, keep food and drinks in separate cool boxes. This is especially important for any meat that you're taking with you – if you take frozen meat and keep it tightly sealed in a cool box, it will keep fresher for longer.

COOKING EQUIPMENT CHECKLIST

- ☐ Double-burner camping stove and/or barbecue
- ☐ Grill rack, charcoal, wood and newspaper for barbecue and/or campfire
- ☐ Lighter or matches
- ☐ Barbecue tongs and metal skewers
- ☐ Large and small heavy-based cooking pots with lids
- ☐ Large nonstick, lidded frying pan
- ☐ Ridged griddle pan (if using a stove)
- ☐ Meat thermometer (optional)
- ☐ Kitchen knife and chopping board
- ☐ Cheese grater
- ☐ Plastic mixing bowl, measuring jug, spoons and colander
- ☐ Pastry brush
- ☐ Rolling pin – not essential, but useful for crushing seeds and rolling pizza dough
- ☐ Can and bottle openers
- ☐ Wooden spoon, spatula and slotted spoon
- ☐ Vegetable peeler
- ☐ Crockery and cutlery
- ☐ Kitchen paper and bin bags
- ☐ Foil, clingfilm and freezer bags
- ☐ Plastic containers with lids
- ☐ Cool box(es) and ice packs
- ☐ Washing-up bowl and liquid
- ☐ Tea towels and oven gloves or mitt

FOOD ESSENTIALS CHECKLIST

- ☐ Vegetable oil and olive oil, for cooking
- ☐ Butter or spread
- ☐ Salt and pepper
- ☐ Tea bags, coffee and sugar
- ☐ Condiments
- ☐ Eggs
- ☐ Cans – beans, tomatoes, fruit
- ☐ Bread
- ☐ Milk
- ☐ Soft drinks
- ☐ Alcohol
- ☐ Onions and garlic
- ☐ Pasta, rice, noodles
- ☐ Crisps and snacks

COOKING METHODS
& Techniques

CAMPFIRE COOKING

If your cosy campfire is also your oven, you need to treat it a little differently; instead of continuously stoking up the logs, you need to let the flames burn down into charcoal so the temperature is white hot and even, and perfect for cooking. Alternatively, you can move the cooking coals over to one side and stoke up the flames on the other. Now you can use a simple campfire grill rack to cook your food directly over the coals.

Alternatively, you can wrap potatoes, fish and meat in sheets of heavy-duty kitchen foil – adding some oil, herbs or other flavourings – and place these directly in the coals. As heat in a campfire is never completely even, make sure you rotate the parcels occasionally so that they cook evenly.

BARBECUE

Some campsites provide designated barbecue areas and you might have a traditional charcoal variety or a gas option. If you're cooking for a large group of people or are preparing a number of dishes, barbecuing might be a better option than the campfire. With charcoal barbecues, the same rules apply as campfire cooking, in that you will need to spark up the coals at least 30 minutes before you plan to start cooking.

CAMPING STOVE

If you need some instant power for a quick plate of egg and beans, a double-burner camping stove offers a convenient way to cook and can also be combined with cooking over coals to get the best of both worlds. It goes without saying that you should make sure you bring enough gas to last the duration of your trip, and test the stove before you leave home to make sure it's in working order, especially if you haven't used it for a while.

A NOTE ON FOOD SAFETY

It takes a bit of practice to master the art of cooking by fire and torchlight. If you want to remain friends with your camping companions, it's imperative to ensure food is fully cooked through before you serve it. Campfires and barbecues have a fairly relaxed temperament when it comes to maintaining temperature so, even though chicken breasts may have been grilling away for hours and are charred on the outside, that's no guarantee that they're cooked in the middle. Cooking times given for the recipes in this book should be used as a guide only – always check food is cooked through and piping hot before you start eating. You could also include a meat thermometer to ensure that barbecued meat is cooked through.

Perfect Pitch

There are various schools of thought when it comes to choosing the perfect place on the campsite to pitch your tent or park up your campervan but, while the highest spot in the site might be one camper's idea of the ultimate prize, it will just as likely be another's exposed wind tunnel of hell. Once you've become a more seasoned camper, you'll probably have your pitch-picking skills honed to perfection, having tried and tested a number of different spots on different sites.

The weather will always be a major factor when choosing your spot, which is why the general thinking is that a flat, raised pitch will see you through the worst that a stormy night can throw at you. However, add a gusty wind into the mix and a pitch perched on raised ground might not be the ideal choice: you'll spend a sleepless night wondering how firm your mallet arm was when you knocked in the tent pegs. Here are a few other factors to consider before staking your claim on a spot.

Shelter - this is especially important if you plan on trying to light an open fire for cooking.

Position - try to set the tent so that the sleeping area faces the setting sun, otherwise you'll be in for an early wake-up call when the sun rises.

Space - if the prime spot is also the smallest, look around for somewhere else. You need some space around your tent or van for cooking, seating, hanging up clothes, etc.

Neighbours - this is down to personal preference: if you like a chat with other campers over your morning cup of tea, set yourself up in a middle pitch; if you want to be at one with nature then search out a more isolated spot.

Families - if you have children it makes sense to pick a pitch near other families: the kids should make friends, giving you some much-needed downtime. Plus, if your children have a meltdown you'll get sympathy rather than dirty looks.

Call of nature - pitching up next to the toilet block isn't everyone's idea of the perfect wilderness weekend but if your bladder can't make it through the night, you might want to keep the conveniences close by.

PREPARE & COOK AHEAD

It's great to prepare big family meals on camping trips. But be realistic about what's achievable when you're preparing dinner in the dark on a small gas stove or over a wood fire. You can save yourself a great deal of time, effort and cursing by preparing a few essentials at home - it's not cheating; think of it more as pre-emptive stress relief.

WEIGH UP

Get organized in advance of your trip and make a meal plan. Measure all the dry ingredients you'll need into sealable plastic freezer bags so you only have to carry what you need. To avoid taking a pestle and mortar, crush any seeds or pods required at home, then transfer to small, lidded containers.

GRATED CHEESE

If you grate and store it in an airtight container you can also dispense with a grater (although a small one is always useful for recipes requiring citrus rind, grated ginger or veg).

BREADCRUMBS

If you're making burgers, it is useful to make fresh breadcrumbs in advance and store them in a sealable plastic freezer bag. Alternatively, make the complete burger mix in advance and store in an airtight container in a cool box for up to 1 day.

MARINATE

To add a bit of extra flavour to meat or fish, it's worth considering marinating it overnight before you set off, then you can arrive, crank up the campfire and have a delicious, flavoursome meal.

PASTA

Cook the pasta of your choice in a large saucepan of lightly salted boiling water for 10 minutes until just tender, drain well, return to the pan and stir through a little olive oil to stop it sticking. Leave to cool, then store in sealable bags. It can be quickly reheated or stirred into a sauce when you're at the campsite.

BAKED POTATOES

These can be cooked in advance, then wrapped in foil and popped on the campfire for an authentic alfresco snack.

BOILED EGGS

Perfect for salads, sandwiches and snacks - cook, cool and peel the eggs before you leave.

SAUCES

A container full of pre-prepared curry or pasta sauce will provide a quick and delicious camping meal. Stir in some veggies or meat and serve with cooked pasta or rice for the first night.

MEAT

Cooked meat can be kept chilled in a cool box for a day and then fully reheated for a quick supper - try chicken pieces for an alfresco curry or barbecue skewers; pulled pork to serve in wraps, buns or baguettes; and drumsticks for a fireside buffet.

MAKE A MEAL OF IT

Pre-prepared one-pot meals like chilli, curry, stew and ratatouille are ideal for camping. You can make batches and keep them frozen in sealed containers in your cool box for up to two days.

BASIC RECIPES

Making a few homemade essentials to take with you ensures you always have the makings of a tasty meal to hand.

Granola

100 g (3½ oz) mixed nuts
spray olive oil, for greasing
200 g (7 oz) porridge oats
1 tablespoon maple syrup

Makes 4 servings
Prep time 5 minutes, plus cooling
Cooking time 15 minutes

1   Fry the nuts in a dry frying pan over a medium-low heat for 3-4 minutes, shaking the pan occasionally, until toasted. Leave to cool, then roughly chop.

2   Spray a baking sheet lightly with spray oil. Put the oats and nuts in a bowl and stir in the maple syrup. Spread the mixture out on the prepared baking sheet and bake in a preheated oven, 180°C (350°F), Gas Mark 4, for 5 minutes.

3   Remove from the oven and stir well. Return to the oven and bake for a further 3-4 minutes until lightly toasted. Leave to cool, then store in an airtight container for up to 1 week.

Hot harissa sauce

1 tablespoon coriander seeds
1 teaspoon caraway seeds
3 tablespoons olive oil
1 red pepper, cored, deseeded and roughly chopped
1 small red onion, roughly chopped
1 red chilli, deseeded and chopped
3 garlic cloves, chopped
4 tablespoons coriander leaves, torn into pieces
½ teaspoon celery salt
150 ml (¼ pint) passata

Serves 4-6
Prep time 10 minutes
Cooking time 5 minutes

1   Using a pestle and mortar, grind the coriander and caraway seeds until lightly crushed. Alternatively, use a small bowl and the end of a rolling pin.

2   Tip the seeds into a frying pan, add the oil, red pepper and onion and cook over a very low heat for 5 minutes, or until the vegetables are soft.

3   Transfer the mixture to a food processor or blender and add the chilli, garlic, coriander leaves, celery salt and passata.

4   Blend until smooth, scraping the mixture down from the sides of the bowl if necessary. Leave to cool, then transfer to an airtight container and store in a cool box for up to 2 days.

Homemade biscuits

150 g (5 oz) medium oatmeal
150 g (5 oz) plain flour, plus extra for dusting
150g (5oz) slightly salted butter, cut into small pieces, plus extra for greasing
75 g (3 oz) light muscovado sugar

Makes about 20 biscuits
Prep time 10 minutes, plus chilling
Cooking time 15 minutes

1   Put the oatmeal and flour in a food processor, add the butter and blend until the mixture resembles coarse breadcrumbs. Add the sugar and mix to a paste. Wrap in clingfilm and chill for 30 minutes.

2   Roll out the dough on a floured work surface to 2.5 mm (1/8 inch) thick and cut out 7 cm (3 inch) rounds with a cutter. Transfer to greased baking sheets, spaced slightly apart, and bake in a preheated oven, 190°C (375°F), Gas Mark 5, for about 15 minutes until pale golden.

3   Transfer to a wire rack and leave to cool. Store in an airtight container for up to 1 week. These can also be used to make S'mores on page 243.

BACON & MAPLE SYRUP PANCAKES

TREACLE & MUSTARD BEANS

POTATO DROP SCONES

PANCAKES WITH BLUEBERRIES

BREAKFASTS

BANANA & CINNAMON PORRIDGE

Herb omelette
WITH MUSTARD MUSHROOMS

IF YOU PREFER, COOK HALF THE EGG MIXTURE AT
A TIME TO MAKE TWO SMALLER OMELETTES.

1 Beat together the mustard and butter in a bowl, then
spread over the undersides of the mushrooms. Put them
mustard side up, on a foil-lined grill rack over a barbecue or
campfire, or in a hot griddle pan, and cook for about 5 minutes,
or until tender.

2 Meanwhile, beat together the herbs and eggs in a jug, then
season with salt and pepper.

3 Melt a knob of butter in a frying pan until foaming, then
swirl in the egg mixture and cook over a medium heat until
just set. Carefully slide the omelette on to a plate, add the
mushrooms and serve.

1 tablespoon wholegrain mustard
3 tablespoons butter, softened,
   plus extra for frying
4 flat mushrooms
2 tablespoons chopped mixed
   fresh herbs (such as chives,
   parsley and tarragon)
4 eggs
salt and pepper

Serves **2**
Prep time **5 minutes**
Cooking time **10 minutes**

CAMPING TIP

Keep your toothbrushes fresh and
clean (and stop them from wetting
the rest of your toiletries once
they have been used) by loosely
wrapping them individually in
kitchen foil after each use.

SMOKED SALMON
Scrambled Eggs

3 large eggs
1 tablespoon milk
a knob of butter, plus extra for
   spreading (optional)
1-2 slices of wholemeal bread
1 tablespoon single cream
   (optional)
25–40 g (1–1½ oz) smoked salmon,
   cut into narrow strips
1 teaspoon finely snipped chives
salt and pepper

Serves **1**
Prep time **10 minutes**
Cooking time **about 5 minutes**

1 Beat the eggs in a jug with a fork. Add the milk and season with salt and pepper.

2 Melt the butter in a frying pan over a low heat until foaming. Pour the eggs into the foaming butter and cook, stirring constantly and scraping the bottom of the pan and bringing the eggs from the outside to the centre. The eggs are done when they form soft, creamy curds and are barely set.

3 Meanwhile, toast the bread in a griddle pan or on a grill rack over a barbecue or campfire. Spread with butter, if liked.

4 Remove the eggs from the heat and stir in the cream, if using, the salmon and chives. Pile on to the hot toast and serve immediately.

TRAFFIC LIGHT
SCRAMBLED EGGS

3 tablespoons olive oil
1 small onion, finely chopped
½ green pepper, cored, deseeded
and roughly chopped
½ red pepper, cored, deseeded
and roughly chopped
½ yellow pepper, cored, deseeded
and roughly chopped
1 garlic clove, crushed
6 eggs, beaten
100 ml (3½ fl oz) single cream
or milk
4 thick slices of wholemeal bread

Serves **4**
Prep time **10 minutes**
Cooking time **10-15 minutes**

1 Heat the oil in a frying pan, add the onion and peppers and cook over a medium heat for about 5 minutes until softened. Add the garlic and cook for a further 1 minute, then add 3 tablespoons water. Cover with a lid or foil and simmer for 2 minutes.

2 Beat together the eggs and cream or milk in a jug. Remove the lid or foil from the pan, pour in the eggs and stir over a low heat with a wooden spoon until the eggs are creamy and just set.

3 Meanwhile, toast the bread in a griddle pan or on a grill rack over a barbecue or campfire. Serve the eggs spooned over the warm toast.

MUSHROOM CRÊPES

1 Put the flour, milk, egg and salt and pepper in a bowl and beat until smooth. Set aside.

2 To make the filling, put all the ingredients in a small saucepan and cook over a medium-low heat for about 5-10 minutes, stirring occasionally, until the mushrooms are softened.

3 Heat a little oil in a frying pan over a medium heat. Pour in a ladleful of the batter and cook for about 1 minute, or until golden underneath. Carefully flip the pancake over and cook on the other side. Slide on to a plate, add a quarter of the mushroom filling, roll up and serve.

4 Repeat with the remaining batter and filling to make 3 more pancakes, adding a little more oil to the pan as required.

50 g (2 oz) plain flour
150 ml (¼ pint) milk
1 small egg; beaten
olive oil
salt and pepper

Filling
300 g (10 oz) chestnut
   mushrooms, chopped
1 bunch of spring onions, finely
   chopped
1 garlic clove, chopped
400 g (13 oz) can chopped
   tomatoes, drained
2 tablespoons chopped oregano

Serves **4**
Prep time **10 minutes**
Cooking time **20 minutes**

CAMPING TIP

Packing up the car can take a long time so try to get as much organized the night before as possible. You should aim to arrive at the campsite early so you have a choice of pitches and a stress-free set-up.

CREAMY
MUSHROOMS
ON TOAST

1 tablespoon olive oil
1 tablespoon lime juice
1 small onion, chopped
8 mushrooms, sliced
1 tablespoon light soy sauce
2 tablespoons ricotta cheese
4 slices of wholemeal bread

Serves **2**
Prep time **5 minutes**
Cooking time **10 minutes**

1 Heat the oil in a frying pan, add the lime juice and fry the onion and mushrooms over a medium heat for about 5 minutes until softened. Stir in the soy sauce and ricotta.

2 Meanwhile, toast the bread in a griddle pan or on a grill rack over a barbecue or campfire.

3 Pour the mushrooms on top of the toast and serve immediately.

BACON *& maple syrup* PANCAKES

300 g (10 oz) plain flour
2½ teaspoons baking powder
½ teaspoon salt
1 egg, lightly beaten
425 ml (14½ fl oz) milk
2 tablespoons butter, melted
olive oil
8 smoked back bacon rashers
maple syrup, to serve

Serves **4**
Prep time **5 minutes**
Cooking time **15–30 minutes**

1 Put the flour, baking powder and salt in a bowl. Make a well in the centre and gradually beat in the egg and milk until smooth. Stir in the melted butter.

2 Heat a little oil in a frying pan over a medium heat. Pour in about 100 ml (3½ fl oz) of the batter and cook for 1–2 minutes, or until bubbles start appearing on the surface. Carefully flip the pancake over and cook for a further 1–2 minutes on the other side until golden. Slide on to a plate, cover with foil and keep warm. Repeat with the remaining batter to make 7 more pancakes, adding a little more oil to the pan as required.

3 Meanwhile, heat a griddle pan over a medium-high heat, add the bacon and cook for about 2 minutes on each side until golden and cooked through.

4 Serve the pancakes topped with the bacon and drizzled with maple syrup.

PANCAKES
WITH **BLUEBERRIES**

125 g (4 oz) plain flour
1 egg
300 ml (½ pint) milk
250 g (8 oz) blueberries
2 tablespoons fresh orange juice
1-2 tablespoons caster sugar,
   to taste
vegetable oil
4 tablespoons crème fraîche,
   to serve (optional)

Serves **4**
Prep time **5 minutes**
Cooking time **30 minutes**

1 Put the flour, egg and milk in a bowl and beat until smooth. Set aside.

2 Place the blueberries, orange juice and sugar, to taste, in a small saucepan over a low heat and warm gently until the blueberries begin to burst. Remove from the heat and leave to cool slightly.

3 Heat a little oil in a frying pan over a medium heat. Pour in a little of the batter, swirl to coat thinly and cook gently for 2 minutes, or until golden underneath. Carefully flip the pancake over and cook on the other side. Slide on to a plate, cover with foil and keep warm. Repeat with the remaining batter to make 7 more pancakes, adding a little more oil to the pan as required.

4 Serve the pancakes with the warm blueberries and dollops of crème fraîche, if liked.

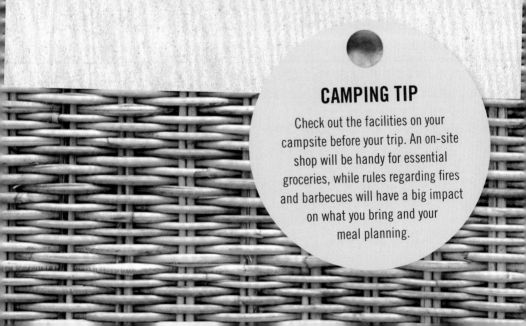

CAMPING TIP

Check out the facilities on your campsite before your trip. An on-site shop will be handy for essential groceries, while rules regarding fires and barbecues will have a big impact on what you bring and your meal planning.

BUTTERMILK
Pancakes

LIGHT, FLUFFY AND DELICIOUS, THESE THICK PANCAKES ARE BEST SERVED
STRAIGHT FROM THE PAN TOPPED WITH A LITTLE BUTTER AND JAM. IF YOU
PREFER TO SERVE ALL THE PANCAKES TOGETHER, KEEP THEM HOT ON A PLATE
COVERED WITH FOIL WHILE YOU COOK THE REMAINING BATTER. IF YOU DON'T
HAVE ANY BUTTERMILK, THEN USE LOW-FAT NATURAL YOGURT MIXED WITH
HALF THE AMOUNT OF MILK INSTEAD.

1 Put the flour, baking powder and bicarbonate of soda in a
bowl and make a well in the centre. Put the egg whites into
a separate clean bowl and beat until they form soft peaks.

2 Add the egg yolks and buttermilk to the flour mixture
and beat until smooth. With a large spoon, fold in the
egg whites.

3 Heat a little oil in a frying pan over a medium heat.
Drop large spoonfuls of the batter into the pan, spacing
them slightly apart, and cook for about 3 minutes, or until the
undersides are golden and the tops are bubbling. Flip the
pancakes over and cook on the other side until cooked through.
Remove from the pan and serve warm with butter and jam.

4 Repeat with the remaining batter, adding a little more
oil to the pan as required.

200 g (7 oz) plain flour
1 teaspoon baking powder
½ teaspoon bicarbonate
  of soda
2 eggs, separated
275 ml (9 fl oz) buttermilk
vegetable oil

To serve
butter
jam

Serves **4**
Prep time **15 minutes**
Cooking time **20 minutes**

COOKING TIP

For the second batch, wipe
the pan with a piece of folded
kitchen paper moistened with
a little oil before adding
the batter.

BANANA & CARDAMOM
PANCAKES

BANANA AND CARDAMOM ARE AN UNBEATABLE COMBINATION, SO IF YOU'RE
TAKING A LOT OF RIPE BANANAS ON YOUR CAMPING TRIP, THIS IS FOR YOU!

1 Mash the bananas in a large bowl, add the flour, sugar, melted butter, milk and egg and beat until smooth. Stir in the cardamom.

2 Heat a little oil in a frying pan over a medium heat. Drop 3-4 tablespoons of the batter into the pan, spacing them slightly apart, and cook for 2-3 minutes. Flip the pancakes over and cook on the other side for a further 2 minutes, or until lightly browned and cooked through. Remove from the pan and serve warm with honey.

3 Repeat with the remaining batter, adding a little more oil to the pan as required.

4 ripe bananas
300 g (10 oz) self-raising flour
2 tablespoons caster sugar
2 tablespoons melted butter
100 ml (3½ fl oz) milk
1 egg, lightly beaten
2 teaspoons crushed cardamom
   seeds
vegetable oil, for frying
honey, to serve

Serves **4**
Prep time **10 minutes**
Cooking time **10-15 minutes**

FRENCH TOASTS
WITH BANANAS, PECANS & CARAMEL

1 egg
1 tablespoon caster sugar
3 tablespoons milk
¼ teaspoon ground cinnamon
2 chunky slices of white or grainy
  bread, crusts removed if liked
2 tablespoons unsalted butter
1 teaspoon vegetable oil
15 g (½ oz) pecan nuts, roughly
  chopped
4 tablespoons caramel sauce
2 small bananas

Serves **2**
Prep time **10 minutes**
Cooking time **15-20 minutes**

1 Beat the egg in a shallow dish, adding the sugar, milk and cinnamon once the egg is broken up. Dip the bread slices in the mixture, turning them over so they've absorbed the batter on both sides.

2 Heat the butter and oil in a frying pan until foaming. Add the bread slices and cook, turning once, until golden on both sides. Transfer to plates.

3 Drain off any oil in the pan and add the pecan nuts. Cook until lightly toasted, shaking the pan frequently. Add the caramel sauce, then the bananas, slicing them into the caramel.

4 Stir for a few minutes to heat through. Spoon the sauce on to the toast and serve.

ORANGE
French Toast

2 oranges
6 slices of raisin bread
2 eggs
50 ml (2 fl oz) milk
¼ teaspoon ground cinnamon
2 tablespoons butter
2 tablespoons vegetable oil
soured cream, to serve (optional)

Serves **4**
Prep time **10 minutes**
Cooking time **10 minutes**

1 Pare the rind from one of the oranges with a lemon zester or sharp knife and set aside. Using a sharp knife, remove the peel and pith from both oranges, then cut between the membranes to separate the segments and set aside.

2 Cut the bread slices in half diagonally. Beat together the eggs, milk and cinnamon in a shallow dish.

3 Heat half the butter and oil in a frying pan until foaming. Quickly dip half the bread triangles in the egg mixture, turning them over so they've absorbed the batter on both sides, then add to the pan. Cook for about 5 minutes, turning once, until golden on both sides. Remove from the pan, cover with foil and keep warm. Repeat with the remaining butter, oil and bread.

4 Top the toast with the orange segments and rind, and serve with dollops of soured cream, if liked.

Potato
DROP SCONES

1 Cook the potatoes in a saucepan of lightly salted boiling water for about 15 minutes, or until completely tender. Drain well, return to the saucepan and mash until smooth. Leave to cool slightly.

2 Beat in the baking powder, then the eggs, milk and a little salt and pepper, and continue to beat until everything is evenly combined.

3 Heat a little oil in a frying pan over a medium heat. Drop heaped spoonfuls of the mixture into the pan, spacing them slightly apart, and fry for about 5 minutes, turning once, until golden on both sides. Remove from the pan and serve warm with griddled bacon and tomatoes, if liked.

4 Repeat with the remaining potato mixture to make 12 drop scones, adding a little more oil to the pan as required.

550 g (1 lb 2 oz) large potatoes, peeled and cut into small chunks
1½ teaspoons baking powder
2 eggs
75 ml (3 fl oz) milk
vegetable oil, for frying
salt and pepper

Serves **4**
Prep time **10 minutes, plus cooling**
Cooking time **25-30 minutes**

Treacle & MUSTARD BEANS

1 Put all the ingredients in a large saucepan over a low heat and bring slowly to the boil, stirring occasionally. Cover with a lid and simmer gently for 1 hour, stirring occasionally. Remove the lid and cook for a further 30 minutes.

2 Towards the end of the cooking time, toast the bread in a griddle pan, or on a grill rack over a barbecue or campfire, for 2 minutes on each side until lightly charred. Rub each bread slice with a peeled garlic clove and drizzle with olive oil.

3 Serve the beans with the garlic-rubbed bread.

1 carrot, diced
1 celery stick, chopped
1 onion, chopped
2 garlic cloves, crushed
2 x 400 g (13 oz) cans soya
   beans, drained
700 g (1 lb 7 oz) jar passata
75 g (3 oz) smoked bacon
   rashers, diced
2 tablespoons black treacle
2 teaspoons Dijon mustard
salt and pepper

To serve
6 thick slices of sourdough
   bread
1-2 garlic cloves, peeled
olive oil, for drizzling

Serves **6**
Prep time **10 minutes**
Cooking time **1 hour 35 minutes**

CULINARY
CAMPING TIPS

Everyone expects to rough it a bit when they're spending their holiday under canvas but that doesn't mean surviving on charred toast and tepid beans for the duration: there are plenty of ways to make mealtimes occasions to look forward to and you don't need to sacrifice too much boot space to do it.

SPICE UP YOUR LARDER

You won't use much in the way of herbs and spices but a little goes a long way and you'll be surprised by the selection you can take with you if you pack carefully. You can decant dried herbs and spices – as well as sauces like ketchup, soy sauce and chilli sauce – into small plastic bottles and containers, taking just the amount you'll need for your trip. These can be used to add instant flavour to everyday meals such as noodles, rice dishes, omelettes, baked potatoes and stews.

CEREAL

As with condiments, there's no point filling up your food containers with big boxes of cereal – measure out the amounts you'll need and put them in smaller containers or sealable plastic bags to save on space. Alternatively, buy individual cereal servings: these also cut down on washing up, as savvy campers can add milk directly to the plastic packaging and use it as a bowl.

MORNING CUPPA

Take as many tea bags as you need (plus a few extra as tea is a staple on camping trips). If you're a coffee drinker, buy sachets of instant coffee rather than taking a whole jar. Do the same with sugar – this will stop it getting damp or attracting ants.

SAY CHEESE

Cheese is a camping essential. A key ingredient in everything from toasties to omelettes and a finishing flourish for pasta dishes, this should be in everyone's store cupboard. Hard cheeses will stay fresh if kept out of the fridge for a few days as long as the temperature doesn't skyrocket. To save time, grate the cheese before you leave home and keep it in an airtight container so it's ready to use when you're cooking.

INSTANT MEALTIME

Pasta and rice can take an age to cook, especially if you're relying on a campfire to get up to speed. Packets of fresh, ready-to-eat rice, pasta and noodles are a camping cook's lifesaver that can help you create a whole range of substantial meals in a matter of minutes – and all in one pot.

BOSTON
Baked Beans

1 tablespoon vegetable oil
1 small red onion, finely chopped
2 celery sticks, finely chopped
1 garlic clove, crushed
200 g (7 oz) canned chopped
  tomatoes
150 ml (¼ pint) vegetable stock
1 tablespoon dark soy sauce
1 tablespoon dark brown sugar
2 teaspoons Dijon mustard
400 g (13 oz) can mixed beans,
  drained
2 tablespoons chopped parsley

Serves **2**
Prep time **10 minutes**
Cooking time **30-40 minutes**

REAL HOMEMADE BAKED BEANS ARE A REVELATION.
SERVE ON TOAST OR WITH SAUSAGES.

1 Heat the oil in a saucepan, add the onion and cook over a medium heat for about 5 minutes until softened. Add the celery and garlic and cook for a further 1-2 minutes.

2 Add the tomatoes, stock and soy sauce. Bring to the boil, then cook at a fast simmer for about 15 minutes, or until the sauce begins to thicken.

3 Add the sugar, mustard and beans. Continue to cook for 5 minutes, or until the beans are heated through. Stir in the chopped parsley and serve.

CAMPING TIP

Finding the right place to pitch is really important. The best spot will have morning shade and evening sunshine. The golden rule is: always choose the most level ground available but never camp on the flat next to a river.

RUSTIC PARMESAN & OLIVE BREAD

1 Put the flour, salt, pepper, yeast, oil and cheese in a bowl and add 275 ml (9 fl oz) hand-hot water. Mix with a round-bladed knife to make a smooth dough, adding a dash more water if the dough is dry. Tip out on to a lightly floured board and knead for about 10 minutes until the dough is smooth and elastic. Work in the olives towards the end of the kneading process. (If you've no surface to work on, work the dough in the bowl as best as you can.) Return the dough to the bowl, cover with a clean tea towel or clingfilm and leave in a warm place (near the fire if already lit) until the dough has doubled in size.

2 Cut a large square of baking parchment and place over a large piece of heavy-duty foil. Punch the dough to deflate it and divide roughly into 16 pieces. Shape each piece into a ball and space slightly apart on the paper. Position the balls in rows so you end up with a rectangular shape. Place on a tray. Bring the foil up around the dough and seal, then leave until the dough has once again doubled in size.

3 Slide the foil parcel on to a grill rack over a barbecue or campfire and cook the bread for about 1 hour, or until it sounds hollow when tapped on the bottom, moving the parcel frequently on the rack so the bread cooks evenly.

4 Carefully remove the breads from the foil parcel. To brown the tops, toast them on a toasting fork over the fire before serving.

450 g (14½ oz) strong white bread flour, plus extra for dusting
1 teaspoon salt
½ teaspoon freshly ground black pepper
2 teaspoons fast-action dried yeast
3 tablespoons olive oil
65 g (2½ oz) Parmesan cheese, grated
75 g (3 oz) pitted black olives, roughly chopped

Serves **8**
Prep time **30 minutes, plus proving**
Cooking time **about 1 hour**

Summer berry GRANOLA

1 Divide the granola between bowls and pour over the milk, then add the berries.

2 Serve with Greek yogurt and a drizzle of maple syrup.

1 quantity of Granola (see page 11)
milk, as required
150 g (5 oz) mixed summer berries

To serve
Greek yogurt
maple syrup

Serves **4**
Prep time **5 minutes**

QUINOA & SULTANA *Porridge*

1 orange
175 g (6 oz) quinoa flakes
475 ml (16 fl oz) milk
75 g (3 oz) sultanas
2 bananas
ground cinnamon (optional)
honey, to serve

Serves **4**
Prep time **10 minutes**
Cooking time **10-15 minutes**

1 Grate the rind of the orange, then peel the orange and segment the flesh. Set aside.

2 Put the quinoa flakes in a saucepan, pour in the milk and 250 ml (8 fl oz) water, and add the sultanas. Bring to the boil over a medium heat, stirring, then simmer over a low heat for 4-5 minutes, stirring frequently, until the quinoa is soft and the porridge thick and creamy.

3 Spoon the porridge into bowls immediately, because it will thicken with standing. Slice the bananas, then divide among the bowls with the orange segments. Sprinkle with the orange rind and a little ground cinnamon, if using. Serve with a drizzle of honey.

Banana & Cinnamon
PORRIDGE

150 g (5 oz) porridge oats
300 ml (½ pint) milk
2 bananas
4 tablespoons light or dark
  muscovado sugar
¼ teaspoon ground cinnamon

Serves **4**
Prep time **5 minutes**
Cooking time **10-15 minutes**

1 Put the oats in a saucepan, pour in the milk and add 600 ml (1 pint) boiling water. Bring to the boil over a medium heat, stirring, then simmer over a low heat for about 5-6 minutes, stirring frequently, until the oats are soft and the porridge thick and creamy.

2 Spoon the porridge into bowls, then slice the bananas and divide among the bowls. Mix together the sugar and cinnamon and sprinkle over the top.

CORNED BEEF HASH

750 g (1½ lb) potatoes, peeled
  and diced
3 tablespoons vegetable oil,
  plus a little extra
1 large onion, chopped
2 garlic cloves, chopped
340 g (11½ oz) can corned beef,
  chopped or crumbled
4 eggs
ketchup, barbecue or brown
  sauce, to serve (optional)

Serves **4**
Prep time **10 minutes**
Cooking time **30 minutes**

1 Cook the potatoes in a large saucepan of boiling water for about 10 minutes until just tender. Drain well.

2 Meanwhile, heat 2 tablespoons of the oil in a frying pan, add the onion and garlic and cook over a medium-low heat for about 7-8 minutes until softened.

3 Add the remaining oil to the pan with the corned beef and drained potatoes and mix well. Continue to cook for about 15 minutes, turning occasionally - but not too often - until crispy and golden. Transfer to a large dish, cover with foil and keep warm while you fry the eggs in the pan with a little extra oil.

4 Spoon the hash on to plates and top with the fried eggs. Serve immediately with sauce, if liked.

SAUSAGE & BACON BURGERS

THESE JUMBO BURGERS SHOULD KEEP HUNGRY
CAMPERS HAPPY. IF YOU ARE FEELING EXTRA
HUNGRY, THEN ADD A FRIED EGG, TOO.

1 Put the sausage meat into a mixing bowl and add the bacon,
spring onions and apple. Sprinkle in the mustard powder and
season well with salt and cayenne pepper. Stir with a spoon until
well combined.

2 Divide the mixture into 4 and shape into burgers using
floured hands. Cover with clingfilm or put into a sealable
plastic bag and chill in a cool box until required.

3 Brush the burgers lightly with the oil and cook on a
grill rack over a hot barbecue or campfire for about
15-20 minutes, turning once or twice, until browned and cooked
through. To double check, make a slit through the centre of one
of the burgers - there should be no hint of pink in the middle.

4 Split the rolls and toast, cut side down, on the rack.
Arrange the tomatoes over the bottom halves, add the
burgers and a spoonful of relish or ketchup, then top with the
lids and serve.

1 tablespoon vegetable oil
4 ciabatta rolls or burger buns
3 tomatoes, sliced
tomato relish or ketchup

Burger mix
500 g (1 lb) good-quality sausages,
    about 8 in total, skins removed
125 g (4 oz) bacon rashers, diced
4 spring onions, finely chopped
1 apple, cored and coarsely grated
    (but not peeled)
1 teaspoon mustard powder
flour, for dusting
salt and cayenne pepper

Serves **4**
Prep time **15 minutes, plus
chilling**
Cooking time **15-20 minutes**

Poached eggs,
BACON & MUFFINS

WHEN CAMPING, POACHING THE EGGS SEPARATELY
ENSURES EACH SERVING IS AS HOT AS POSSIBLE.

8 back or streaky bacon rashers
2 tablespoons chopped basil
2 tablespoons olive oil
4 tomatoes, thickly sliced
4 muffins
4 large eggs
1 tablespoon vinegar
butter, for spreading
salt and pepper

Serves **4**
Prep time **5 minutes**
Cooking time **20 minutes**

1 Heat a frying pan over a medium heat, then add the bacon rashers and dry-fry for about 6-8 minutes, turning once, until cooked through. Push to the side of the pan.

2 Mix together the basil and oil in a bowl. Add the tomato slices to the frying pan and drizzle over the basil oil. Season well with salt and pepper, then cook for 3-4 minutes until starting to soften.

3 Meanwhile, split the muffins and toast in a griddle pan or on a grill rack over a barbecue or campfire. Wrap in a clean tea towel and keep warm.

4 Bring a large saucepan of water to the boil. Break 1 of the eggs into a cup, making sure not to break the yolk. Add the vinegar to the boiling water, then stir the water rapidly in a circular motion to make a whirlpool. Carefully slide the egg into the centre of the pan while the water is still swirling, holding the cup as close to the water as you can. Cook for about 3 minutes, then lift out with a slotted spoon.

5 Butter 2 halves of a muffin. Top the bottom half with a quarter of the tomato slices, 2 rashers of bacon and the poached egg, then top with the lid and serve.

6 Cook and serve the other 3 eggs in the same way, swirling the boiling water into a whirlpool each time before sliding in the egg.

BBQ & CAMPFIRE

40 CLASSIC HAMBURGERS

41 FAST-SEARED STEAKS WITH FRENCH BEANS

42 THAI CHILLI BEEF BURGERS

44 SUGAR & SPICE GLAZED BEEF

45 GREEN PEPPERCORN STEAKS

46 BUTTERFLIED LEG OF LAMB WITH BROAD BEAN & DILL YOGURT

47 AROMATIC BARBECUED LAMB

47 TAVERNA-STYLE LAMB WITH FETA SALAD

48 MINTED LAMB KEBABS

49 BARBECUED PORK SPARE RIBS

50 PORK ESCALOPES WITH LEMON & CAPERS

51 STICKY GAMMON STEAKS WITH CARAMELIZED ONIONS

52 CHORIZO & QUAIL'S EGG PIZZAS

53 SEARED PORK CHOPS WITH CHILLI CORN

54 SPIT-ROASTED PORK WITH APPLE BUTTER

55 CHICKEN SATAY SKEWERS

56 LEMON & PARSLEY CHICKEN SKEWERS

57 TANDOORI CHICKEN SKEWERS WITH CUCUMBER & CUMIN SALAD

58 BLACKENED CHICKEN SKEWERS

59 CHICKEN BURGERS WITH TOMATO SALSA

60 CHICKEN & MOZZARELLA SKEWERS

62 HERB-MARINATED SPATCHCOCK CHICKEN

63 SPIT-ROASTED CHICKEN WITH SAFFRON MAYONNAISE

64 CHICKEN FAJITAS

66 THAI BARBECUED CHICKEN

67 PRAWN & BACON SKEWERS

68 SCALLOP & CHORIZO SKEWERS

69 QUICK TUNA STEAKS WITH GREEN SALSA

70 BLACKENED TUNA WITH MANGO SALSA

72 SWORDFISH STEAKS WITH BASIL & PINE NUT OIL

73 OLIVE & CITRUS SALMON

74 STUFFED SALMON FILLETS WITH PANCETTA & TOMATOES

75 MACKEREL WITH CITRUS FENNEL SALAD

TOMATO, PESTO & OLIVE PIZZAS

SALT & PEPPER
TIGER PRAWNS

PORK SPARE RIBS

CLASSIC HAMBURGERS

olive oil, for brushing
4 burger buns
2 tablespoons mustard
shredded lettuce
2 tomatoes, sliced
2 dill pickles, sliced

Burger mix
500 g (1 lb) rib-eye steak,
  minced
250 g (8 oz) skinless pork belly,
  minced
1 onion, finely chopped
1 teaspoon Worcestershire
  sauce
2 tablespoons capers, drained
salt and pepper

Serves **4**
Prep time **10 minutes, plus
chilling**
Cooking time **10-12 minutes**

1 Put the beef mince, pork mince, onion, Worcestershire
sauce, capers, salt and pepper in a bowl. Mix together well,
using your hands. Divide the mixture into 4 and shape into
even-sized burgers. Cover with clingfilm or put in a sealable
plastic bag and chill in a cool box for 30 minutes.

2 Brush the burgers lightly with oil and cook on a grill rack
over a hot barbecue or campfire for about 5-6 minutes on
each side, or until lightly charred and cooked through.

3 Meanwhile, split the buns and toast on both sides on the
rack. Spread the bottom halves with a little mustard, then
fill with the shredded lettuce, burgers, tomato slices and dill
pickles. Top with the lids and serve.

FAST-SEARED STEAKS
WITH **FRENCH BEANS**

1 Cook the green beans in a saucepan of lightly salted boiling water for about 2-3 minutes, or until tender but firm.

2 Meanwhile, to make the tomato dressing, mix together all the ingredients in a bowl.

3 Drain the beans and return to the pan. Toss the tomato dressing through the beans, season well with salt and pepper, cover with a lid and keep warm.

4 Rub the oil over the steaks, then cook on a rack over a hot barbecue or campfire for 1 minute on each side, or until cooked to your liking. Transfer to a plate, cover with foil and leave to rest for 1-2 minutes.

5 Divide the rocket salad on to plates. Spoon over the beans and dressing, then top with the steaks. Serve immediately with crusty bread.

400 g (13 oz) green beans, trimmed
1 teaspoon olive oil
4 thin steaks (such as feather steaks or frying steaks)
200 g (7 oz) rocket salad
salt and pepper
crusty bread, to serve

Tomato dressing
2 tomatoes, diced
1 teaspoon olive oil
1 banana shallot, finely chopped
1 tablespoon wholegrain mustard
1 tablespoon red wine vinegar

Serves **4**
Prep time **10** minutes
Cooking time **5 minutes**

THAI *Chilli Beef* BURGERS

olive oil, for brushing
1 baguette, cut into 4 and split
   lengthways
shredded lettuce
sweet chilli sauce

Burger mix
500 g (1 lb) minced beef
1 tablespoon Thai red curry
   paste
25 g (1 oz) fresh white
   breadcrumbs
2 tablespoons chopped fresh
   coriander
1 egg, lightly beaten
1 tablespoon light soy sauce
pepper

Serves 4
Prep time **10 minutes**
Cooking time **10 minutes**

1 Put the minced beef in a bowl and stir in the red curry paste, breadcrumbs, coriander, egg, soy sauce and pepper. Mix together well using your hands. Divide the mixture into 8 and shape into mini burgers.

2 Brush the burgers lightly with oil and cook on a grill rack over a hot barbecue or campfire for about 4-5 minutes on each side, or until charred and cooked through.

3 Serve the burgers in the split bread with shredded lettuce and sweet chilli sauce.

SUGAR & SPICE GLAZED BEEF

8 juniper berries
3 tablespoons black treacle
2 tablespoons light muscovado sugar
2 tablespoons whisky
2 tablespoons Worcestershire sauce
1 tablespoon grainy mustard
½ teaspoon finely ground black pepper
600 g (1¼ lb) piece of fillet steak
salt

Serves 4-5
Prep time **10 minutes, plus marinating**
Cooking time **about 30 mins**

1 Crush the juniper berries using a pestle and mortar. Mix in a bowl with the treacle, sugar, whisky, Worcestershire sauce, mustard and pepper. Put the steak in a non-metallic dish and pour the marinade all over the surface. Cover loosely with clingfilm and leave to marinate in your cool box for about 1 hour.

2 Lift the meat from the dish, letting the excess marinade drip back into the dish and season with a little salt. Transfer to a grill rack over a barbecue or campfire and cook for about 30 minutes, turning the meat frequently so it cooks fairly evenly. Use a meat thermometer to test whether the beef is cooked to your liking. For rare the temperature should register about 50°C (120°F). For well done, the meat should register 70-75°C (158-165°F) and will take longer to cook.

3 Pour the marinade juices into a small saucepan and heat through on the rack beside the meat. Transfer the meat to a board and carve into thick slices. Serve with the juices drizzled over.

CAMPING TIP

If the weather forecast is for rain, the golden rule of pitching on flat ground can be wavered and you should pitch your tent on a slight incline or on the highest part of the site so it doesn't flood — there's nothing worse than waking up in a soggy sleeping bag.

Green PEPPERCORN STEAKS

1 Heat a griddle pan on a grill rack over a hot barbecue or campfire until very hot.

2 Meanwhile, cook the steaks on the grill rack for 2-3 minutes on each side, or until cooked to your liking. Transfer to a plate, cover with foil and leave to rest while you make the sauce.

3 Put the peppercorns, soy sauce, balsamic vinegar and cherry tomatoes in the griddle pan. Leave the liquids to sizzle for a few minutes, or until the tomatoes are soft. Spoon the sauce over the steaks and serve.

4 lean fillet steaks, about 75 g (3 oz) each
1 tablespoon green peppercorns in brine, drained
2 tablespoons light soy sauce
1 teaspoon balsamic vinegar
8 cherry tomatoes, halved

Serves 4
Prep time 5 minutes
Cooking time about 10 minutes

BUTTERFLIED
LEG OF LAMB
with Broad Bean & Dill Yogurt

5 garlic cloves, crushed
4 handfuls of mint leaves,
  chopped
4 handfuls of parsley, chopped
3 tablespoons green
  peppercorns in brine, drained
  and crushed
2 tablespoons olive oil
1 butterflied leg of lamb, about
  1.75 kg (3½ lb) in total

Broad bean and dill yogurt
100 g (3½ oz) fresh baby broad
  beans
200 ml (7 fl oz) Greek yogurt
4 tablespoons chopped dill
salt

Serves 6
Prep time **15 minutes, plus
marinating**
Cooking time **about 30-40
minutes**

1 Mix together the garlic, mint, parsley, peppercorns and oil.
Open out the lamb and spread the herb mixture all over
the surface of the lamb. Place in a non-metallic dish and
cover loosely with clingfilm. Leave to marinate for several
hours or overnight in the cool box, allowing the meat to sit at
room temperature for a couple of hours before cooking.

2 To make the yogurt, cook the beans in a saucepan of
boiling water for 3-5 minutes until tender. Drain and
leave to cool. Pop the beans out of their skins and mix with
the yogurt, dill and a little salt. Transfer to a serving dish.

3 Transfer the lamb to a grill rack over a hot barbecue or
campfire and cook for 15-20 minutes on each side, or
until thoroughly browned on the outside but still pink in the
middle.

4 Place on a serving board or plate, cover with foil and
leave to rest for 15 minutes before slicing. Serve with
the yogurt.

COOKING TIP

Cook the meat where the heat
is least intense and for longer
if you prefer lamb cooked
through.

AROMATIC **BARBECUED** LAMB

1 Place the lamb chops in a shallow, non-metallic dish. Mix the ginger with the garlic, chilli, sugar, soy sauce and sherry and pour it over the lamb.

2 Turn the meat in the mixture, cover with cllingfilm and chill in a cool box for at least 2 hours or overnight.

3 Transfer the chops to a grill rack over a hot barbecue or campfire and cook for 3-8 minutes on each side, depending on whether you like the meat rare or well done. Use any excess marinade to baste the meat while it is cooking.

4 Serve with baked new potatoes.

4 lamb chump chops
2 cm (3/4 inch) piece of fresh root ginger, peeled and grated
2 garlic cloves, crushed
1 red chilli, deseeded and thinly sliced
2 teaspoons dark muscovado sugar
3 tablespoons soy sauce
2 tablespoons dry sherry
Fire-baked New Potatoes (see page 203), to serve

Serves **4**
Prep time **10 minutes**
Cooking time **about 10-15 minutes**

Taverna-Style LAMB WITH FETA SALAD

2 tablespoons chopped oregano
1 tablespoon chopped rosemary
grated rind of 1 lemon
2 tablespoons olive oil
salt and pepper
500 g (1 lb) leg or shoulder of lamb, diced
crusty bread, to serve (optional)

Feta salad
200 g (7 oz) feta cheese, sliced
1 tablespoon chopped oregano
2 tablespoons chopped parsley
grated rind and juice of 1 lemon
1/2 small red onion, finely sliced
3 tablespoons olive oil

1 Mix together the herbs, lemon rind, oil and salt and pepper in a non-metallic dish, add the lamb and mix to coat thoroughly. Thread the meat on to 4 metal skewers.

2 Arrange the sliced feta on a large serving dish and sprinkle over the herbs, lemon rind and sliced onion. Drizzle over the lemon juice and oil and season with salt and pepper.

3 Cook the lamb skewers on a grill rack over a hot barbecue or campfire for about 6-8 minutes, turning frequently until charred on the outside and almost cooked through. Transfer to a plate, cover with foil and leave to rest for 1-2 minutes.

4 Serve the lamb, with any pan juices poured over, with the salad and plenty of crusty bread, if liked.

Serves **4**
Prep time **15 minutes**
Cooking time **about 8 minutes**

MINTED LAMB KEBABS

500 g (1 lb) minced lamb
1 small onion, finely chopped
1 garlic clove, crushed
1 tablespoon chopped rosemary
6 anchovies in oil, drained and
  chopped
olive oil, for brushing
salt and pepper

Tomato and olive salad
6 tomatoes, cut into wedges
1 red onion, sliced
125 g (4 oz) pitted black olives
a few torn basil leaves
2 tablespoons olive oil
a squeeze of lemon juice

1 Put the lamb, chopped onion, garlic, rosemary, anchovies and some salt and pepper in a bowl and mix together using your hands. Divide the mixture into 12 and shape into even-sized, sausage-shaped patties. Cover with clingfilm and chill in the cool box for 30 minutes.

2 Thread the patties on to metal skewers, brush lightly with oil and cook on a grill rack over a hot barbecue or campfire for about 3-4 minutes on each side, or until cooked through.

3 Meanwhile, to make the salad, put the tomatoes, onion, olives and basil in a bowl, season with salt and pepper and mix together. Drizzle with oil and squeeze a little lemon juice over. Serve the kebabs with the salad.

Serves **4**
Prep time **15 minutes, plus chilling**
Cooking time **about 7 minutes**

BARBECUED PORK
spare ribs

100 ml (3½ fl oz) tomato
   ketchup
2 tablespoons clear honey
1 tablespoon dark soy sauce
1 tablespoon olive oil
1 tablespoon malt vinegar
2 teaspoons Dijon mustard
4 x 500 g (1 lb) packs pork
   spare ribs
salt and pepper

Serves **4**
Prep time **5 minutes**
Cooking time **about 20-30
minutes**

1 Mix together all the ingredients except the pork in a bowl, then coat the ribs generously all over with the marinade.

2 Transfer to a grill rack over a barbecue or campfire and cook for about 20-30 minutes, basting occasionally with the marinade and turning frequently, until charred and tender.

PORK ESCALOPES
WITH LEMON & CAPERS

1 tablespoon chopped flat leaf parsley

3 tablespoons chopped mint

4-6 tablespoons lemon juice

1 tablespoon capers, drained and chopped

6 tablespoons olive oil, plus extra for brushing

4 pork escalopes, about 125 g (4 oz) each, trimmed

1 Mix together the herbs, lemon juice, capers and oil in a bowl.

2 Brush the pork with oil and cook on a grill rack over a hot barbecue or campfire for about 2-3 minutes on each side, or until cooked through.

3 Drizzle the lemon and caper dressing over the pork and serve.

Serves **4**
Prep time **10 minutes**
Cooking time **about 5 minutes**

CAMPING TIP

Bring collapsible fabric garden or clothes bins for flexible storage while you're on site. They can be used for shoes and wellies, firewood or keeping the tent clutter free. And they barely take up any space once they're folded away.

Sticky GAMMON STEAKS WITH CARAMELIZED ONIONS

1 Melt the butter in a frying pan, add the onions and thyme leaves and cook over a low heat, stirring occasionally, for about 15 minutes until softened and beginning to caramelize. Stir in the marmalade, mustard and stock and bring to the boil, then simmer gently for 2-3 minutes until beginning to thicken.

2 Meanwhile, brush the gammon steaks with the oil and cook on a grill rack over a barbecue or campfire for about 15 minutes, turning once, until cooked through.

3 Add the steaks to the sauce and simmer for a further 3 minutes until the sauce is thick and sticky and the steaks are piping hot. Serve with instant mash, if liked.

a knob of butter
2 onions, sliced
2 teaspoons thyme leaves
4 tablespoons thick-cut marmalade
1 tablespoon wholegrain mustard
300 ml (½ pint) hot chicken stock
4 lean gammon steaks, about 100 g (3½ oz) each
1 tablespoon olive oil
instant mashed potato, to serve (optional)

Serves **4**
Prep time **5 minutes**
Cooking time **25 minutes**

CHORIZO
& Quail's Egg PIZZAS

150 g (5 oz) strong white bread flour, plus extra for dusting
½ teaspoon fast-action dried yeast
½ teaspoon salt
1 tablespoon olive oil

Topping
2 tablespoons olive oil, plus extra for drizzling
1 small garlic clove, crushed
75 g (3 oz) thinly sliced chorizo sausage
1 red chilli, deseeded and halved
100 g (3½ oz) Manchego cheese, grated
2 tablespoons pine nuts
6 quail's eggs
salt and pepper
rocket leaves, to scatter

Serves **2**
Prep time **25 minutes, plus proving**
Cooking time **about 30 minutes**

1 To make the pizza base, mix the flour, yeast, salt and olive oil in a bowl and add 75 ml (3 fl oz) hand-hot water. Mix with a round-bladed knife to make a soft dough, adding a dash more water if the dough is dry. Tip out on to a floured board and knead for about 10 minutes until the dough is smooth and elastic. (If you've no surface to work on, knead the dough in the bowl as best as you can.) Return the dough to the bowl, cover with a clean tea towel or clingfilm and leave in a warm place (near the fire if already lit) until the dough has doubled in size.

2 Heat a pizza spatula, pizza stone or sturdy baking sheet on a rack over a barbecue or campfire while assembling the pizza. Mix together the olive oil and garlic in a bowl.

3 Turn the dough out on to a floured surface and cut in half. Thinly roll out each piece to an oval shape measuring about 22 x 14 cm (8½ x 5½ inches) or to a size that allows you to fit them side by side on the baking sheet or pizza spatula or stone. Transfer to the baking sheet or pizza stone and brush with the garlic oil. Scatter with the chorizo and add a chilli half to each. Sprinkle with the cheese and pine nuts and make 3 small indentations in each topping, then break the eggs into the wells and season with salt and pepper.

4 Make a dome of foil and position over the pizzas, tucking the ends under the base to secure. Cook for about 30 minutes, or until the bases are cooked and the eggs are softly set. Rotate the pizzas on the rack several times during cooking. Serve scattered with rocket leaves and an extra drizzle of oil.

Seared PORK CHOPS
WITH CHILLI CORN

1 Brush the chops with half the oil and cook on a grill rack over a barbecue or campfire for about 5-10 minutes on each side (depending on thickness), or until golden and cooked through. Keep warm and allow to rest for 5 minutes.

2 Meanwhile, to make the chilli corn, heat the remaining oil in a frying pan, add the sweetcorn and cook for 2 minutes until starting to brown, then stir in the spring onions and chilli and cook for a further 1 minute. Add the créme fraîche and lime rind and season to taste with salt and pepper. Scatter over the coriander and serve with the pork chops.

2 tablespoons olive oil
4 pork chops
200 g (7 oz) canned sweetcorn kernels
2 spring onions, thinly sliced
1 red chilli, chopped
5 tablespoons créme fraîche
finely grated rind of 1 lime
handful of coriander leaves, chopped
salt and pepper

Serves **4**
Prep time **10 minutes**
Cooking time **10-20 minutes**

Spit-Roasted Pork
WITH APPLE BUTTER

IF YOU DON'T HAVE SPIT-ROASTING EQUIPMENT, ROAST THE PORK ON A GRILL RACK OVER THE FIRE, TURNING IT FREQUENTLY UNTIL COOKED THROUGH. WRAP THE JOINT IN FOIL TO FINISH COOKING IF IT STARTS TO BURN.

1 Mix together the fennel seeds, caraway seeds, garlic, lemon rind, pepper and a little salt in a bowl. Make plenty of cuts over the surface of the meat with the tip of a knife, then push some of the spice mixture into the cuts and spread the remainder all over the surface. Roll up and tie the pork at 3 cm (1¼ inch) intervals with kitchen string.

2 Skewer the pork on to a spit-roasting rod and set up over a campfire or barbecue. Roast for about 3-4 hours, or until the pork is cooked through. Test the pork is cooked by pushing a meat thermometer into the thickest area of the meat. It should read about 75°C (165°F).

3 To make the butter, chop the apples into pieces and put in a saucepan with a dash of water. Cover with a lid and cook on the rack to one side of the pork until the apples are tender. You'll need to frequently add more water to stop the apples burning on the base of the pan before they're soft. Once soft and mushy, remove from the heat, stir in the cloves, sugar and lemon juice and leave to cool. Add the butter to the cooled apple mixture and beat well to mix.

4 Transfer the pork to a plate or board. Cover with foil and leave to rest in a warm place near the barbecue or fire for 15 minutes before removing the string. Carve into thick slices and serve in baps, baguettes or soft wraps with the apple butter.

2 teaspoons fennel seeds, lightly crushed
2 teaspoons caraway seeds, lightly crushed
4 garlic cloves, crushed
finely grated rind of 2 lemons
1 teaspoon freshly ground black pepper
2 kg (4 lb) shoulder of pork, skin and excess fat removed
salt
baps, baguettes or soft wraps, to serve

Apple butter
500 g (1 lb) cooking apples, peeled, quartered and cored
pinch of ground cloves
1 teaspoon caster sugar
squeeze of lemon juice
4 tablespoons very soft slightly salted butter

Serves 6
Prep time **25 minutes**
Cooking time **3-4 hours**

CHICKEN SATAY
SKEWERS

1 Soak 8 wooden skewers in cold water for 30 minutes. Mix together the soy sauce, oil and 5-spice powder in a bowl. Add the chicken strips and toss together to coat in the marinade. Cover with clingfilm and leave to marinate in the cool box for 1 hour, stirring occasionally.

2 Thread the chicken, zigzag fashion, on to the soaked skewers. Transfer to a grill rack over a hot barbecue or campfire and cook for about 10 minutes, turning once, until golden and cooked through.

3 Meanwhile, put the sauce ingredients in a small saucepan with 8 tablespoons water and heat, stirring, until warm and well mixed. Transfer to a small serving bowl.

4 Serve the hot chicken skewers with the satay sauce and cucumber strips.

6 tablespoons dark soy sauce
2 tablespoons vegetable oil
1 teaspoon Chinese 5-spice powder
2-3 boneless, skinless chicken breasts, about 375 g (12 oz) in total, cut into long, thin strips
cucumber, cut into strips, to serve

Satay sauce
4 tablespoons peanut butter
1 tablespoon dark soy sauce
½ teaspoon ground coriander
½ teaspoon ground cumin
pinch of paprika or chilli powder

Serves **4**
Prep time **20 minutes, plus marinating**
Cooking time **10 minutes**

Lemon & Parsley
CHICKEN SKEWERS

2 boneless, skinless chicken
  breasts, about 300 g (10 oz)
  in total, cut into chunks
finely grated rind and juice of
  1 lemon
2 tablespoons olive oil
3 tablespoons finely chopped
  parsley
salt and pepper

To serve
rocket and tomato salad
warm pitta breads
200 g (7 oz) tub tzatziki

Serves **2**
Prep time **15 minutes**
Cooking time **10-15 minutes**

1 Put the chicken in a bowl with the lemon rind and juice and
the oil and toss well to coat. Stir in the parsley and season
well with salt and pepper.

2 Thread the chicken on to 4 small metal skewers. Transfer
to a grill rack over a hot barbecue or campfire and
cook for about 10-15 minutes, turning once, until golden and
cooked through.

3 Remove from the skewers and serve in warm pitta breads
with a simple rocket and tomato salad and spoonfuls
of tzatziki.

TANDOORI CHICKEN SKEWERS
with cucumber & cumin salad

175 g (6 oz) Greek yogurt,
  plus extra to serve
2 tablespoons tandoori paste
3-4 boneless, skinless chicken
  breasts, about 500 g (1 lb)
  in total, cut into thin strips
2 lemons, cut into wedges
mini naan breads, to serve
  (optional)

Cucumber salad
2 teaspoons cumin seeds
1 small cucumber
1 red onion, cut in half and finely
  sliced
3 tablespoons coriander leaves
salt and pepper

Serves 4
Prep time **15 minutes, plus
marinating**
Cooking time **12 minutes**

1 Mix together the yogurt and tandoori paste in a bowl, add the chicken and toss until the chicken is well coated. Cover with clingfilm and leave to marinate for 10 minutes.

2 Heat a frying pan over a medium heat, add the cumin seeds and dry-roast for 1-2 minutes, stirring frequently. Remove from the heat when the seeds become fragrant and begin to smoke.

3 Thread the chicken strips on to 8 small metal skewers. Transfer to a grill rack over a hot barbecue or campfire and cook for about 10 minutes, turning once, until cooked through.

4 Meanwhile, slice the cucumber into ribbons using a sharp vegetable peeler and arrange on plates. Scatter the onion and coriander over the cucumber, sprinkle over the toasted cumin seeds and season lightly with salt and pepper. Place the chicken on top and serve with lemon wedges, extra yogurt and warm naan breads, if liked.

BLACKENED
CHICKEN
SKEWERS

2 boneless, skinless chicken
  breasts, about 300 g (10 oz),
  cut into chunks
1 tablespoon Cajun seasoning
  mix
2 tablespoons lemon juice
1 teaspoon olive oil

To serve
Garlic Bread (see page 206)
green salad

Serves **4**
Prep time **5 minutes, plus
marinating**
Cooking time **10-15 minutes**

1 Soak 8 wooden skewers in cold water for 30 minutes. Put the chicken in a bowl, add the seasoning mix, lemon juice and olive oil and toss together well. Cover with clingfilm and leave to marinate for 15 minutes.

2 Thread the chicken on to the soaked skewers. Transfer to a grill rack over a hot barbecue or campfire and cook for about 10-15 minutes, turning once, until cooked through.

3 Serve with garlic bread and a green salad.

CAMPING TIP

Washing powder is good for cleaning your barbecue. Simply mix a couple of tablespoons of powder into some hot water and scrub off the remains of last night's sausage feast. If you have a large container, you can soak the grill rack in the liquid overnight to soften the grease and the results will be even better.

CHICKEN BURGERS
WITH TOMATO SALSA

1 Mix together all the burger ingredients except the oil in a bowl. Divide the mixture into 4 and shape into even-sized flattened rounds. Cover with clingfilm and chill in a cool box for 30 minutes.

2 Meanwhile, combine all the tomato salsa ingredients together in a bowl.

3 Brush the burgers lightly with the oil and cook on a grill rack over a hot barbecue or campfire for about 3-4 minutes on each side, or until cooked through. Serve immediately with the salsa.

1 garlic clove, crushed
3 spring onions, finely sliced
1 tablespoon ready-made pesto
2 tablespoons chopped fresh
 mixed herbs (such as parsley,
 tarragon and thyme)
375 g (12 oz) minced chicken
2 sun-dried tomatoes, finely
 chopped
1 teaspoon olive oil

Tomato salsa
250 g (8 oz) cherry tomatoes,
 quartered
1 red chilli, cored, deseeded and
 finely chopped
1 tablespoon chopped fresh
 coriander
grated rind and juice of 1 lime

Serves **4**
Prep time **15 minutes, plus
chilling**
Cooking time **6-8 minutes**

CHICKEN & MOZZARELLA SKEWERS

8 small boneless, skinless
chicken thigh fillets
2 bocconcini balls (baby
mozzarellas), quartered
8 large basil leaves
8 large slices of prosciutto
2 small lemons, halved
salt and pepper

Serves 4
Prep time **15 minutes**
Cooking time **20 minutes**

1 Lay the chicken thighs flat on a plate, boned side up, and
season with a little salt and pepper. Place a quarter of a
bocconcini and a basil leaf in the centre of each, then roll up to
enclose the filling. Wrap each thigh in a slice of prosciutto and
thread on to 8 metal skewers, using 2 skewers for 2 parcels
(this makes them easier to turn).

2 Transfer the skewers to a grill rack over a hot barbecue
or campfire and cook for about 8 minutes on each side, or
until cooked through and the mozzarella starts to ooze. Transfer
to a plate, cover with foil and leave to rest for 5 minutes.

3 Meanwhile, cook the lemon halves, cut side down, for
5 minutes until charred and tender. Serve the skewers
drizzled with the lemon juice.

HERB-MARINATED
Spatchcock Chicken

1 teaspoon cumin seeds, lightly crushed
2 garlic cloves, crushed
2 handfuls of parsley, chopped
2 handfuls of coriander leaves, chopped
¼ teaspoon dried chilli flakes
1 tablespoon vegetable oil
1 tablespoon clear honey
finely grated rind of 1 lemon
2 teaspoons lemon juice
1 whole chicken, about 1.5 kg (3 lb)
salt

To serve
leafy salad
new potatoes

Serves **4**
Prep time **20 minutes, plus marinating**
Cooking time **about 40 minutes**

1 Mix together the cumin seeds, garlic, parsley, coriander, chilli flakes, oil, honey and lemon rind and juice in a bowl.

2 To spatchcock the chicken, place the chicken on a board, breast side down. Using sturdy kitchen scissors, cut along one side of the backbone, then the other to remove the backbone completely. Turn the bird over, breast side up, and flatten out the legs so they face inwards. Use the heel of your hand to push the breastbone firmly down and flatten out the chicken completely.

3 Push a wooden skewer diagonally through the bird so the skewer goes through one leg then out through the wing on the other side. Push another skewer through in the opposite direction. Spread the herb mixture over the chicken on both sides and place on a plate. Cover loosely with clingfilm and leave to marinate in a cool box for several hours.

4 Season the chicken lightly with salt on both sides. Transfer to a grill rack over a barbecue or campfire and cook for about 20 minutes on each side, or until the juices run clear when the thickest part of the chicken is pierced with a sharp knife. If the chicken skin starts to burn before the chicken is cooked through, wrap it in foil and move to one side of the rack so it can cook more gently.

5 Transfer the chicken to a large board or plate, cover with foil and leave to rest for 5 minutes, then chop the chicken into pieces and serve with salad and new potatoes.

SPIT-ROASTED CHICKEN
WITH SAFFRON MAYONNAISE

IF YOU DON'T HAVE SPIT-ROASTING EQUIPMENT, ROAST THE CHICKEN ON A GRILL RACK OVER A BARBECUE OR CAMPFIRE, TURNING IT FREQUENTLY UNTIL COOKED THROUGH. IF THE SKIN STARTS TO BURN, WRAP THE CHICKEN IN FOIL TO FINISH COOKING. SPATCHCOCKING THE CHICKEN FIRST (SEE PAGE 62) WILL HELP SPEED UP COOKING TIME.

1 Put the paprika, fennel seeds, celery seeds, garlic and pepper in a large plastic freezer bag and shake the bag to mix the ingredients together. Add the chicken to the bag. Balloon out the bag, twisting the open end to secure, and turn the chicken in the spice mixture until coated. Tie loosely and leave to marinate in a cool box for several hours or overnight.

2 Push the herbs into the chicken cavity. Skewer the chicken on to a spit-roasting rod and set up over a campfire or barbecue. Sprinkle with a little salt and roast for about 1½-2 hours, or until the chicken is cooked through. The juices should run clear when the thickest part of the thigh is pierced with the tip of a sharp knife.

3 To make the mayonnaise, crumble the saffron into a mug and add 1 teaspoon boiling water. Leave to stand for 5 minutes. Beat the crème fraîche and mayonnaise together in a bowl with a little salt and pepper. Stir in the saffron and liquid.

4 Transfer the chicken to a plate or board and cover with foil. Leave to rest in a warm place near the barbecue or fire for 15 minutes before carving. Serve with the mayonnaise.

2 teaspoons ground paprika
1 teaspoon fennel seeds, lightly crushed
½ teaspoon celery seeds
2 garlic cloves, finely chopped
½ teaspoon freshly ground black pepper
1 whole chicken, about 1.5 kg (3 lb)
small handful of bay leaves, thyme and parsley
salt

Saffron mayonnaise
good pinch of saffron strands
100 ml (3 fl oz) crème fraîche
100 g (3 oz) mayonnaise

Serves 4
Prep time **15 minutes, plus marinating**
Cooking time **about 1½-2 hours**

½ teaspoon ground coriander
½ teaspoon ground cumin
½ teaspoon ground paprika
1 garlic clove, crushed
3 tablespoons chopped fresh
  coriander
2-3 boneless, skinless chicken
  breasts, about 375 g (12 oz) in
  total, cut into bite-sized strips
1 tablespoon olive oil
4 soft flour tortillas
soured cream, to serve
  (optional)

Salsa

3 large ripe tomatoes, finely
  chopped
3 tablespoons chopped fresh
  coriander
⅛ cucumber, finely chopped
1 tablespoon olive oil

Guacamole

1 large avocado, peeled, stone
  removed and roughly chopped
grated rind and juice of ½ lime
2 teaspoons sweet chilli sauce
  (optional)

Serves 4
Prep time **20 minutes**
Cooking time **about 5 minutes**

CHICKEN FAJITAS

1 Put all the ground spices, garlic and chopped coriander in a bowl. Toss the chicken in the oil, then add to the spices and toss to coat lightly in the spice mixture. Cover with clingfilm and leave to marinate while you make the salsa.

2 To make the salsa, mix together the tomatoes, coriander and cucumber in a bowl and drizzle over the oil.

3 To make the guacamole, in a separate bowl, mash together the avocado, lime rind and juice and sweet chilli sauce, if using, until soft and rough-textured.

4 Heat a griddle pan or frying pan on a grill rack over a barbecue or campfire until hot, add the chicken and cook for about 5 minutes, turning occasionally, until golden and cooked through.

5 Fill the tortillas with the hot chicken strips, guacamole and salsa. Fold into quarters and serve with a little soured cream, if liked.

THAI BARBECUED
CHICKEN

1 whole chicken, about 1.5 kg (3 lb), spatchcocked (see page 62)
5 cm (2 inch) piece of fresh galangal or root ginger, peeled and finely chopped
4 garlic cloves, crushed
1 large red chilli, finely chopped
4 shallots, finely chopped
2 tablespoons finely chopped fresh coriander
150 ml (1/4 pint) canned coconut milk
salt and pepper

To serve
sweet chilli sauce
lime wedges
boiled rice

Serves **4**
Prep time **20 minutes, plus marinating**
Cooking time **about 40 minutes**

1 Rub the chicken all over with salt and pepper and place in a shallow dish. Mix together the remaining ingredients in a jug until well blended, then pour over the chicken. Cover loosely with clingfilm and leave to marinate in a cool box for several hours or overnight.

2 Transfer the chicken from the marinade to a grill rack over a hot barbecue or campfire and cook for about 20 minutes on each side, turning and basting frequently with the remaining marinade, until the juices run clear when the thickest part of the chicken is pierced with a sharp knife. If the chicken skin starts to burn before the chicken is cooked through, wrap it in foil and move to one side of the rack so it can cook more gently.

3 Transfer the chicken to a large board or plate, cover with foil and leave to rest for 5 minutes, then chop it into small pieces. Serve with sweet chilli sauce, lime wedges and boiled rice.

COOKING TIP

If you prefer, use 4 part-boned chicken breasts. Follow the recipe instructions above, but cook the chicken for only about 10–15 minutes, or until cooked through.

PRAWN & BACON
SKEWERS

1 Soak 12 wooden skewers in cold water for 30 minutes. Cut each bacon rasher into 3 pieces crossways, then run the back of a knife along the length of each piece to stretch them out thinly.

2 Wrap each prawn carefully with bacon and thread on to a soaked skewer with a tomato and basil leaf. Season each skewer with a little salt and pepper.

3 Brush the skewers with a little oil and cook on grill rack over a hot barbecue or campfire for 2–3 minutes on each side, or until the prawns turn pink and are cooked through. Serve hot with the lemon wedges for squeezing over.

4 streaky bacon rashers, rind removed
12 raw peeled large prawns, deveined but tails intact
12 cherry tomatoes
12 basil leaves
olive oil, for brushing
salt and pepper
lemon wedges, to serve

Serves 4
Prep time 10 minutes, plus soaking
Cooking time 4–6 minutes

SCALLOP & CHORIZO SKEWERS

12 scallops, white meat only
12 large sage leaves
150 g (5 oz) chorizo sausage,
    cut into 12 x 1 cm (½ inch)
    pieces
2 tablespoons olive oil
1 tablespoon lemon juice
1 garlic clove, crushed
salt and pepper
lemon wedges, to serve

Serves 4
Prep time **10 minutes, plus
soaking and marinating**
Cooking time **4-6 minutes**

1 Soak 12 small wooden skewers in cold water for 30 minutes. Wrap each scallop with a sage leaf and thread on to the soaked skewers with the pieces of chorizo, then transfer to a dish.

2 Mix together the oil, lemon juice, garlic and salt and pepper in a bowl, then drizzle over the skewers. Cover with clingfilm and leave to marinate in a cool box for 1 hour.

3 Cook the skewers on a grill rack over a hot barbecue or campfire for 2-3 minutes on each side, or until the scallops are cooked though. Serve hot with lemon wedges for squeezing over.

QUICK TUNA STEAKS
with green salsa

2 tablespoons olive oil
grated rind of 1 lemon
2 teaspoons chopped parsley
½ teaspoon crushed coriander
   seeds
4 tuna steaks, about 150 g
   (5 oz) each
salt and pepper
crusty bread, to serve

Salsa
2 tablespoons capers, drained
   and chopped
2 tablespoons chopped
   cornichons
1 tablespoon finely chopped
   parsley
2 teaspoons chopped chives
2 teaspoons finely chopped
   chervil
30 g (1 oz) pitted green olives,
   chopped
1 shallot, finely chopped
   (optional)
2 tablespoons lemon juice
2 tablespoons olive oil

Serves **4**
Prep time **15 minutes**
Cooking time **2-4 minutes**

1 Mix together the oil, lemon rind, parsley, coriander seeds and plenty of pepper in a bowl. Rub the tuna steaks with the mixture and set aside.

2 To make the salsa, mix together the ingredients in a bowl, season to taste with salt and pepper and set aside.

3 Cook the tuna on a grill rack over a hot barbecue or campfire for 1-2 minutes on each side, or until well charred on the outside but still pink in the middle. Alternatively, cook for a little less time, or for longer, until cooked to your liking.

4 Transfer the tuna to a plate, cover with foil and leave to rest for a few minutes. Serve with the salsa and plenty of fresh crusty bread.

4 tuna steaks, about 250 g
   (8 oz) each
1 tablespoon olive oil
2 tablespoons freshly crushed
   black peppercorns
1 teaspoon salt
lime wedges, to serve

Mango salsa
1 large mango, about 500 g
   (1 lb), peeled, stoned and
   diced
½ red onion, finely chopped
1 large red chilli, deseeded and
   finely chopped
1 tablespoon lime juice
2 tablespoons chopped fresh
   coriander
salt and pepper

Serves 4
Prep time **10 minutes, plus
standing**
Cooking time **2-4 minutes**

BLACKENED TUNA WITH MANGO SALSA

1 To make the mango salsa, mix together all the ingredients in a bowl and season to taste with salt and pepper. Leave to stand to allow the flavours to develop.

2 Brush the tuna steaks with a little oil and season with the peppercorns and salt. Cook on a grill rack over a hot barbecue or campfire for about 1-2 minutes on each side, or until well seared on the outside but still pink in the middle. Alternatively, cook for a little less time, or for longer, until cooked to your liking.

3 Transfer the tuna to a plate, cover with foil and leave to rest for a few minutes, then serve with the salsa and lime wedges for squeezing over.

SWORDFISH STEAKS
WITH BASIL & PINE NUT OIL

1 teaspoon olive oil
4 swordfish steaks, about 150 g
  (5 oz) each
250 g (8 oz) herby baby leaf
  salad
75 g (3 oz) ready-to-eat, slow-
  roasted tomatoes, roughly
  chopped
salt and pepper

Basil and pine nut oil
1 small bunch of basil, leaves
  stripped
5 teaspoons olive oil
1 tablespoon toasted pine nuts
1 tablespoon lemon juice

Serves 4
Prep time **15 minutes**
Cooking time **5-7 minutes**

1 Brush the oil over the swordfish steaks and season well with
  salt and pepper. Cook on a grill rack over a barbecue or
campfire for about 5-7 minutes, turning once, until nicely
charred on the outside but still slightly pink in the middle.

2 Meanwhile, to make the basil oil, crush all the ingredients
  in a pestle and mortar, then season with salt and pepper.
Alternatively, finely chop the basil and pine nuts and mix
together with the oil and lemon juice.

3 Pile the baby leaf salad on to plates and scatter with the
  slow-roasted tomatoes. Transfer the swordfish to the plates
and serve with a little basil oil drizzled over.

Olive & Citrus Salmon

1 Remove any stray bones from the salmon fillets. Place the fish on 4 large pieces of heavy-duty foil and top each with a quarter of the olives, tomatoes, oil, lemon and honey. Season with salt and pepper, then bring the foil up around the fish and seal well.

2 Cook the parcels on a grill rack over a hot barbecue or campfire for about 8-10 minutes, or until the fish is cooked through, then transfer to a plate and leave to rest for a few minutes.

3 Carefully open the parcels, sprinkle with chopped parsley and serve with tabbouleh.

4 salmon fillets, about 200 g (7 oz) each
12 large black olives, pitted and halved
12 cherry tomatoes, halved
4 tablespoons olive oil
2 lemon wedges, thinly sliced
2 teaspoons clear honey
salt and pepper
chopped parsley, to garnish
Tabbouleh (see page 208), to serve

Serves **4**
Prep time **5 minutes**
Cooking time **about 8-10 minutes**

Stuffed Salmon Fillets
WITH PANCETTA & TOMATOES

3 shallots, thinly sliced
3 garlic cloves, finely chopped
100 g (3½ oz) sun-dried
  tomatoes in oil, drained and
  chopped
3 tablespoons chopped
  tarragon
2 x 500 g (1 lb) skinless salmon
  fillets
6 thin streaky bacon or
  pancetta rashers
salt and pepper

Serves 5-6
Prep time 15 minutes
Cooking time 40-60 minutes

1 Mix together the shallots, garlic, sun-dried tomatoes, tarragon and a little salt and pepper in a bowl.

2 Remove any stray bones from the salmon fillets. Place one fillet, skinned side up, on a board and spread the shallot mixture on top. Cover with the remaining salmon fillet, skinned side down. Space the bacon or pancetta rashers across the salmon, tucking any long ends underneath. Tie kitchen string around the salmon to hold to the fillets together and secure the bacon rashers in place.

3 Brush a grill rack with oil and place over a barbecue or campfire fire. Cook the salmon for 20-30 minutes on each side, or until cooked through, turning the fish over several times to check that it's not burning on the underside.

4 Transfer to a board or plate and cut away the string. Serve in chunky slices.

CAMPING TIP

If you have to take your tent down when it's blowing a gale, remove the poles first and leave the pegs until last. That way it won't end up turning into a giant parachute and flying off over the horizon.

MACKEREL
WITH *Citrus Fennel* SALAD

1 Slash each mackerel 3-4 times on each side with a sharp knife. Brush with a little oil and season inside and out with salt and pepper. Using kitchen string, tie 3 lemon slices on each side of the fish.

2 Brush with a little more oil and cook on a grill rack over a hot barbecue or campfire for 4-5 minutes on each side, or until lightly charred and cooked through. Cover with foil and leave to rest for 5 minutes.

3 Toss together the fennel slices and fronds, garlic, capers, oil, parsley and lemon juice in a bowl, then season to taste with salt and pepper. Serve the mackerel with the fennel salad.

4 mackerel, about 400 g
(13 oz) each
olive oil, for brushing
3 lemons, thinly sliced

Fennel salad
1 fennel bulb, trimmed and
thinly sliced, fronds
reserved
1 small garlic clove, crushed
2 tablespoons capers,
drained
2 tablespoons olive oil
1 tablespoon chopped parsley
2 tablespoons lemon juice
salt and pepper

Serves **4**
Prep time **20 minutes**
Cooking time **8-10 minutes**

MACKEREL FILLETS
WITH *Pickled Beetroot*

175 g (6 oz) fresh beetroot, grated
3 tablespoons finely chopped dill
2 shallots, finely chopped
2 teaspoons white wine vinegar
1 teaspoon caster sugar
4 small mackerel fillets
salt and pepper
a knob of butter, cubed

Herb yogurt
4 tablespoons Greek yogurt
2 tablespoons finely chopped parsley
squeeze of lemon juice

Serves **2**
Prep time **15 minutes**
Cooking time **20-30 minutes**

1 Mix together the beetroot, dill, shallots, vinegar, sugar and a little salt and pepper in a bowl. Put 2 mackerel fillets on a board, skin side down, and spread the beetroot mixture on top. Place the remaining fillets, skin side up, on top to sandwich the filling.

2 Transfer the stuffed fillets to 2 large squares of heavy-duty foil and dot with the butter, then bring the foil up around the fish and seal well. Tuck between hot coals or logs to cook for about 20-30 minutes, or until the mackerel is cooked through. Rotate the parcels once or twice during cooking.

3 Meanwhile, beat the yogurt, parsley, lemon juice and a little salt and pepper in a bowl. Serve with the fish.

CHARGRILLED SARDINES
with mango & lime salsa

1 Crush together the ginger, lime rind and juice, coriander, oil and chilli in a pestle and mortar to make a rough paste.

2 Score small slits into the sardine flesh, then rub the paste all over, massaging it into the slits.

3 Cook the sardines on a grill rack over a hot barbecue or campfire for about 3-4 minutes on each side, or until cooked through and slightly blackened.

4 Meanwhile, to make the salsa, mix together all the ingredients in a small bowl. Serve with the sardines.

1 teaspoon peeled and finely grated fresh root ginger
finely grated rind and juice of 1 lime
1 small bunch of coriander, roughly chopped
1 tablespoon vegetable oil
½ large red chilli, deseeded and chopped
12-16 fresh sardines, scaled, gutted and cleaned

Mango and lime salsa
1 firm, ripe mango, peeled, stoned and diced
4 tomatoes, deseeded and diced
1 spring onion, finely chopped
2 tablespoons lime juice
½ large red chilli, deseeded and chopped

Serves **4**
Prep time **20 minutes**
Cooking time **6-8 minutes**

SALT & PEPPER TIGER PRAWNS
WITH BABY CORN & MANGO SALSA

1 Mix together the sea salt, Chinese 5-spice powder and black, Szechuan and cayenne peppers in a large bowl, then tip in the prawns and toss until well coated in the spices.

2 Heat a griddle pan over a barbecue or campfire until very hot, arrange the prawns over the pan and cook for about 4-5 minutes, or until the prawns turn pink and are cooked through but still juicy.

3 Meanwhile, to make the baby corn and mango salsa, mix together the baby corn, spring onions, red chilli and diced mango in a bowl, then stir in the sweet soy sauce.

4 Serve the prawns with the tortillas and the baby corn and mango salsa (and a large bowl for the shells).

1 teaspoon coarse sea salt
1 teaspoon Chinese 5-spice powder
1 teaspoon cracked black pepper
½ teaspoon Szechuan peppercorns, crushed
pinch of cayenne pepper
500 g (1 lb) raw tiger prawns, with shells on, rinsed
8 soft flour tortillas, to serve

Baby corn and mango salsa
200 g (7 oz) baby corn, sliced into small rounds
2 spring onions, trimmed and finely chopped
1 chilli, deseeded and finely chopped
1 small mango, peeled, stoned and diced
2 tablespoons sweet soy sauce (ketjap manis)

Serves **4**
Prep time **15 minutes**
Cooking time **about 5 minutes**

PRAWNS
with PIRI PIRI

1 Mix together the oil, lemon rind and juice, piri piri seasoning, tomato purée, garlic and salt and pepper in a bowl. Add the prawns and toss until evenly coated. Cover with clingfilm and leave to marinate in a cool box for at least 2 hours.

2 Thread the prawns on to 12 metal skewers through the thickest part of the body and tail. Transfer to a grill rack over a hot barbecue or campfire and cook for about 5-6 minutes, turning once, until the prawns turn pink and are cooked through.

3 Sprinkle the prawns with chopped parsley and serve with lemon wedges for squeezing over.

3 tablespoons olive oil
grated rind and juice of 1 lemon
2 teaspoons piri piri seasoning
2 teaspoons tomato purée
2 garlic cloves, finely chopped
400 g (13 oz) raw tiger prawns, shells on and heads removed, rinsed
salt and pepper
chopped parsley, to garnish
lemon wedges, to serve

Serves 6
Prep time **15 minutes**, **plus marinating**
Cooking time **5-6 minutes**

CAMPING TIP

If you're planning on having a cheeky tipple while you camp, make sure you bring screw-top bottles of wine and ring-pull cans of lager. Corkscrews and bottle openers tend to go astray and are particularly hard to find after dark when the drinking begins in earnest.

GRILLED SARDINES
with tomato salsa

3 fresh sardines, about 125 g
  (4 oz) in total, scaled, gutted
  and cleaned
4 tablespoons lemon juice
2 slices of ciabatta bread
salt and pepper
1 tablespoon chopped basil,
  to garnish

Tomato salsa
8 cherry tomatoes, chopped
1 spring onion, sliced
1 tablespoon chopped basil
½ red pepper, cored, deseeded
  and chopped

Serves 1
Prep time **10 minutes**
Cooking time **6-8 minutes**

1 To make the tomato salsa, mix together all the ingredients in a bowl.

2 Place the sardines on a plate, drizzle with the lemon juice and season with salt and pepper. Transfer to a grill rack over a hot barbecue or campfire and cook for about 3-4 minutes on each side, or until cooked through.

3 Meanwhile, toast the bread on the rack until lightly charred.

4 Sprinkle the sardines with the chopped basil and serve immediately with the tomato salsa and toasted ciabatta.

ALL ABOUT THE
CAMPFIRE

Our love affair with campfires began the day cave dwellers discovered that rubbing two sticks together for long enough produced fire (along with a fistful of blisters). Since then, this method for keeping warm, scaring off wild beasts and turning unpalatable raw meat into something tasty and safe for consumption has been a global hit. Modern man has wholeheartedly adopted this cooking technique – in the form of the barbecue – to bond with nature and exert his masculinity... with modern woman standing close by with a fire bucket and a plate of spare steaks.

Camping offers the ideal opportunity to explore your hunter-gatherer alter ego and get back to basics. The campfire is the heart of the camping experience, drawing people together to socialize, enjoy the warmth and sizzle a frankfurter or two.

LIGHTING THE FIRE

If your campsite site sells wood, buy some – it will probably be dried out and ready to burn, instead of the collection of damp branches you'll find if you go out gathering your own. You'll need some small twigs, grass or newspaper to get the fire going and you should make a pile of this in the centre, then build up a tentlike structure of bigger kindling and logs around it. Light the kindling and (hopefully) watch as your campfire comes to life.

A FIRE FOR ALL OCCASIONS

If your fire is purely an atmospheric addition to the evening, then you can keep adding logs to fuel the flames. However, a cooking fire requires the logs to burn down into charcoal so the heat is even and hot enough to cook food (see page 8 for campfire cooking techniques).

PUTTING OUT THE FIRE

When the last of the wine has been consumed and it's time to call it a night and crawl into your tent, you need to be meticulous about putting out the campfire. You should gradually let the wood burn down about half an hour before you anticipate the end of the evening. Once the flames have disappeared, you should sprinkle a little water all over the embers and spread them out so that you can make sure the fire has completely extinguished.

POTATO & CHEESE BURGERS

750 g (1½ lb) red or waxy
potatoes, unpeeled
200 g (7 oz) mild Cheddar
cheese, grated
1 red onion, finely chopped
2 tablespoons butter
salt and pepper

To serve (optional)
smoked trout fillets
cucumber slices

Serves **6**
Prep time **10 minutes, plus
cooling**
Cooking time **30 minutes**

1 Cook the potatoes in a large saucepan of boiling water for about 20 minutes, or until just cooked but firm. Drain and leave to cool.

2 Peel the potatoes and grate them into a bowl. Stir in the grated cheese and chopped onion and season with salt and pepper. Divide the mixture into 6 and shape into rounds using wet hands, then press down with two fingers to form into burgers. Neaten up the edges.

3 Melt half the butter in a griddle pan or frying pan over a barbecue or campfire, add half the burgers and cook for about 5 minutes, turning once, until golden brown and heated through. Transfer to a plate, then repeat with the remaining butter and burgers.

4 Serve the burgers warm or cold with lightly smoked trout fillets and cucumber slices, if liked.

Cheddar BURGERS
WITH CUCUMBER SALSA

200 g (7 oz can) butter beans,
  drained
1 onion, finely chopped
1 carrot, grated
100 g (3½ oz) mature Cheddar
  cheese, grated
100 g (3½ oz) fresh
  breadcrumbs
1 egg
1 teaspoon cumin seeds
vegetable oil, for frying
4 round French rolls
salt and pepper

Cucumber salsa
½ small cucumber
2 tablespoons chopped fresh
  coriander
2 spring onions, finely chopped
1 tablespoon lemon or lime juice
1 teaspoon caster sugar

Serves 4
Prep time **15 minutes**
Cooking time **8 minutes**

1 Place the butter beans in a bowl and lightly mash with a fork. Add the onion, carrot, cheese, breadcrumbs, egg, cumin seeds and salt and pepper and mix until evenly combined.

2 Divide the mixture into 4 and shape into small flat cakes. Heat a little oil in a griddle pan or frying pan over a barbecue or campfire and cook the burgers for about 8 minutes, turning once, until crisp, golden and heated through.

3 Meanwhile, for the salsa, halve the cucumber, scoop out the seeds and finely chop. Toss in a bowl with the coriander, spring onions, lemon or lime juice, sugar and a little salt and pepper.

4 Split the rolls and fill with the burgers and salsa.

MUSHROOM, COUSCOUS
& HERB SAUSAGES

1 Put the couscous in a heatproof bowl and add 75 ml (3 fl oz) boiling water. Cover with clingfilm and leave to stand for 5 minutes, then fluff up with a fork.

2 Meanwhile, heat the olive oil in a frying pan, add the onion, mushrooms and chilli and fry over a high heat for about 5 minutes until the mushrooms are golden and the moisture has evaporated.

3 Turn into a bowl, add the remaining ingredients and couscous and mix well. Divide the mixture into 12 and shape into sausage shapes using lightly floured hands. Cover with clingfilm and chill in a cool box for 30 minutes.

4 Brush the sausages with a little oil and cook on a grill rack over a barbecue or campfire for about 10 minutes, turning frequently, until golden and piping hot in the middle.

75 g (3 oz) couscous
3 tablespoons olive oil, plus extra for brushing
1 onion, finely chopped
250 g (8 oz) chestnut mushrooms, finely chopped
1 red chilli, deseeded and finely sliced
3 garlic cloves, finely chopped
small handful of mixed herbs (such as thyme, rosemary and parsley), finely chopped
200 g (7 oz) whole cooked chestnuts, finely chopped
75 g (3 oz) fresh breadcrumbs
1 egg yolk
flour, for dusting
salt and pepper

Serves **4**
Prep time **15 minutes, plus chilling**
Cooking time **10 minutes**

TOMATO, PESTO & OLIVE *Pizzas*

250 g (8 oz) strong white bread flour, plus extra for dusting
½ teaspoon salt
1 teaspoon fast-action dried yeast
1 tablespoon olive oil, plus extra for brushing and drizzling

Topping
2 tablespoons ready-made pesto
200 g (7 oz) cherry tomatoes, halved
150 g (5 oz) mozzarella cheese, sliced
50 g (2 oz) pitted black olives, halved
handful of basil leaves
salt and pepper

Serves **2**
Prep time **30 minutes, plus proving**
Cooking time **20-24 minutes**

1 To make the pizza base, mix the flour, salt and yeast in a bowl. Make a well in the centre, add 125 ml (4 fl oz) hand-hot water and the oil and mix with a round-bladed knife until the mixture comes together in a ball. Tip out on to a floured board and knead for about 10 minutes until the dough is smooth and elastic. (If you've no surface to work on, work the dough in the bowl as best as you can.) Return the dough to the bowl, cover with a clean tea towel or clingfilm and leave in a warm place (near the fire if already lit) until doubled in size.

2 Punch the dough to deflate it, then cut in half. Roll out one piece on a floured board to a round about 23 cm (9 inches) in diameter. Lightly brush a heavy-based frying pan with oil and press the dough into the base. Spread half the pesto over the dough and top with half the tomatoes, mozzarella and olives, some salt and pepper and a drizzle more oil.

3 Place the pan on a grill rack over a moderately hot barbecue or campfire, make a dome of foil and position over the pizza, tucking the ends under the base to secure. Cook for 10-12 minutes until the base is crisp underneath and the cheese melted. Carefully slide the pizza out on to a board, sprinkle with half the basil leaves and serve hot. Repeat with the remaining ingredients to make the second pizza.

DOUBLE CHEESE *Margherita* PIZZA

275 g (9 oz) strong white bread flour, plus extra for dusting
1 teaspoon fast-action dried yeast
1 teaspoon salt
2 tablespoons olive oil

Topping
225 g (7½ oz) can chopped tomatoes
2 tablespoons sun-dried tomato paste
1 teaspoon caster sugar
1 small garlic clove, crushed
250 g (8 oz) mozzarella cheese, thinly sliced
75 g (3 oz) Parmesan cheese, grated
handful of pitted black olives
salt and pepper

Serves 4
Prep time **25 minutes, plus proving**
Cooking time **about 30 minutes**

1 To make the pizza base, mix the flour, yeast, salt and olive oil in a bowl and add 175 ml (6 fl oz) hand-hot water. Mix with a round-bladed knife to make a soft dough, adding a dash more water if the dough feels dry. Tip out on to a floured board and knead for about 10 minutes until the dough is smooth and elastic. (If you've no surface to work on, work the dough in the bowl as best as you can.) Return the dough to the bowl, cover with a clean tea towel or clingfilm and leave in a warm place (near the fire if already lit) until doubled in size.

2 Heat a pizza spatula, pizza stone or sturdy baking sheet on a rack over the fire while assembling the pizza. Turn the dough out on to a floured board and roll out to a round about 30 cm (12 inches) in diameter. Transfer to the baking sheet, stone or spatula.

3 Mix together the tomatoes, tomato paste, sugar, garlic and a little salt and pepper and spread over the base to about 1 cm (½ inch) from the edges. Arrange the mozzarella slices on top and scatter with the Parmesan. Sprinkle with the olives and season with salt and pepper. Make a dome of foil and position over the pizza, tucking the ends under the base to secure. Cook for about 30 minutes, or until the base is cooked and the cheese is melting.

COOKING TIP

You can add your favourite toppings to the basic pizza above. Try a scattering of capers, chopped anchovies, fresh herbs, cherry tomatoes, chopped artichokes, sliced pepperoni or diced crispy bacon. Chargrilled vegetables such as peppers, courgettes, aubergines, mushrooms and asparagus (cooked on over a barbecue or campfire before the pizza) are also delicious.

INDIAN SPICED
SWEET POTATOES

1 Cut the potatoes across into 1 cm (½ inch) thick slices and place in the centres of 4 large squares of heavy-duty foil.

2 Mix together the coconut, cardamom, garlic, chilli and 2 tablespoons of the coriander in a bowl. Spoon the mixture over the potatoes and drizzle with the oil. Bring the foil up around the filling and seal well.

3 Tuck the parcels between hot coals or logs to cook. This will take 1-2 hours depending on the intensity of the fire. Rotate the parcel several times during cooking so the potatoes cook evenly.

4 Carefully open the parcels and serve scattered with the remaining coriander.

800-900 g (1 lb 10 oz-1 lb 14 oz) sweet potatoes, scrubbed
25 g (1 oz) firm creamed coconut, grated
8 cardamom pods, crushed to release the seeds
2 garlic cloves, finely chopped
1 small hot chilli, deseeded and finely chopped
3 tablespoons chopped fresh coriander
2 tablespoons vegetable oil
salt

Serves **4**
Prep time **15 minutes**
Cooking time **1-2 hours**

ONE POT

STEAK & ALE CASSEROLE

VEGETABLE & TOFU STIR-FRY

COCONUT DHAL & TOASTED NAAN FINGERS

BEEF, PUMPKIN & GINGER STEW

2 tablespoons plain flour
750 g (1½ lb) lean stewing beef,
 diced
2 tablespoons butter
3 tablespoons olive oil
1 onion, chopped
2 carrots, sliced
2 parsnips, sliced
3 bay leaves
several thyme sprigs
2 tablespoons tomato purée
625 g (1¼ lb) pumpkin, peeled,
 deseeded and cut into small
 chunks
1 tablespoon dark muscovado
 sugar
50 g (2 oz) fresh root ginger,
 peeled and finely chopped
small handful of parsley,
 chopped, plus extra to garnish
salt and pepper

1 Put the flour on a plate and season with salt and pepper, then coat the beef in the flour. Heat the butter and oil in a large saucepan and fry the meat in two batches until browned, transferring the browned meat to a plate with a slotted spoon.

2 Add the onion, carrots and parsnips to the saucepan and fry gently for 5 minutes. Return the meat to the pan and add the herbs and tomato purée. Add just enough water to cover the ingredients and bring slowly to the boil. Cover with a lid and cook over a low heat, simmering very gently for 45 minutes.

3 Add the pumpkin, sugar, ginger and parsley, re-cover and cook for a further 30 minutes, or until the pumpkin is soft and the meat is tender. Adjust the seasoning if necessary and serve scattered with extra parsley.

Serves **6**
Prep time **20 minutes**
Cooking time 1½ **hours**

QUICK CHILLI TACOS

1 Heat the oil in a large saucepan, add the onion and garlic and cook over a medium heat for about 5 minutes until softened. Add the minced beef and fry for a further 5 minutes, breaking it up with a wooden spoon, until browned.

2 Stir in the passata, beans, chilli sauce and salt and pepper to taste and bring to the boil. Cover with a lid and simmer over a medium-low heat for 15 minutes, stirring occasionally, until thickened.

3 Spoon the chilli on to the tortillas and serve with the cheese, soured cream and coriander.

2 tablespoons olive oil
1 large onion, finely chopped
2 garlic cloves, crushed
500 g (1 lb) lean minced beef
700 g (1 lb 7 oz) jar passata
400 g (13 oz) can red kidney
  beans, drained
2-3 tablespoons hot chilli sauce
salt and pepper

To serve
8 soft corn tortillas, warmed
125 g (4 oz) Cheddar cheese,
  grated
125 g (4 oz) soured cream
handful of fresh coriander
  sprigs

Serves **4**
Prep time **5 minutes**
Cooking time **30 minutes**

COOKING TIP

To warm tortillas, pitta breads and naans, place on a grill rack over a hot barbecue or campfire, or in a frying pan over a high heat, for about 30–60 seconds on each side.

Easy Campfire
BEEF CHILLI

1 tablespoon vegetable oil
1 large onion, chopped
500 g (1 lb) minced beef
400 g (13 oz) can chopped
   tomatoes
4 tablespoons sweet chilli
   sauce
1 tablespoon ground paprika
400 g (13 oz) can red kidney
   beans, drained
squeeze of lemon juice
salt and pepper

To serve
1 small avocado
1 small tomato, finely diced
soured cream
Garlic Bread (see page 206)

Serves **4**
Prep time **15 minutes**
Cooking time **about 1¼
hours**

1 Heat the oil in a large saucepan. Add the onion and cook for about 5 minutes until softened. Add the minced beef and fry for a further 5-10 minutes, breaking it up with a wooden spoon, until lightly browned.

2 Add the canned tomatoes, 3 tablespoons of the chilli sauce and the paprika and heat until simmering. Cover with a lid and cook gently for 20-30 minutes until thick and pulpy. Stir in the kidney beans and lemon juice and cook for a further 15 minutes until heated through.

3 Meanwhile, to make a simple salsa, peel, stone and finely dice the avocado. Put in a bowl with the tomato and remaining chilli sauce and mix together.

4 Serve the chilli with the soured cream, salsa and garlic bread.

STEAK & ALE
Casserole

2 tablespoons plain flour
1 kg (2 lb) braising steak,
    cut into chunks
2 tablespoons butter
1 tablespoon olive oil
2 onions, chopped
2 celery sticks, sliced
several thyme sprigs
2 bay leaves
400 ml (14 fl oz) strong ale
300 ml (½ pint) beef stock
2 tablespoons black treacle
500 g (1 lb) parsnips, cut into
    wedges
salt and pepper
crusty bread, to serve

Serves 5-6
Prep time 20 minutes
Cooking time 1¾ hours

1 Put the flour on a plate and season with salt and
pepper, then coat the beef in the flour. Heat the butter
and oil in a large saucepan and fry the beef in batches until
deep brown, transferring the browned meat to a plate with
a slotted spoon.

2 Add the onions and celery to the pan and cook for
about 5 minutes until softened. Return the beef to the
pan and add the herbs, ale, stock and treacle. Bring just to
the boil, then cover with a lid and simmer gently for 1 hour.

3 Add the parsnips to the pan, re-cover and cook for a
further 30 minutes, or until the beef and parsnips are
tender. Adjust the seasoning if necessary and serve with
crusty bread.

SPICED BEEF & ONION
CHAPPATIS

1 Put the beef, sliced onion, spices and 1 tablespoon of the oil in a bowl and toss well to coat, then season with salt and pepper.

2 Heat the remaining oil in a frying pan, add the red onion wedges and cook over a medium heat for about 2-3 minutes, or until softened. Add the beef and sliced onion and cook for 1-2 minutes on each side, or until golden and cooked through.

3 Spoon the beef and onions on to one side of each chapatti, top with the lime pickle and salad leaves, then fold over to enclose the filling and serve.

300 g (10 oz) thin-cut beef
    frying steak, thinly sliced
1 small onion, thinly sliced
1 teaspoon ground cumin
½ teaspoon ground paprika
½ teaspoon ground coriander
2 tablespoons olive oil
1 red onion, cut into slim wedges
2 soft brown chappatis, warmed
2 tablespoons lime pickle
2 handfuls of salad leaves
salt and pepper

Serves **2**
Prep time **10 minutes**
Cooking time **about 10 minutes**

CAMPING TIP

If you're cooking over a fire, make sure your campsite allows campfires. There may well be assigned spots for setting fire to sticks, or you might have a fire pit or barbecue area next to your pitch. It might sound obvious, but make sure there's plenty of clear space around the fire.

CALVES' LIVER & Bacon

CALVES' LIVER IS THE PRIME CHOICE FOR PAN-FRYING WITH BACON, ALTHOUGH LAMBS' LIVER IS A GOOD SUBSTITUTE. FRY THE LIVER A LITTLE LONGER IF YOU PREFER IT COOKED THROUGH BUT TAKE CARE NOT TO COOK IT FOR TOO LONG OR IT WILL START TO TOUGHEN UP.

plain flour, to coat
625 g (1¼ lb) calf's liver
2 tablespoons butter
1 tablespoon olive oil
12 large sage leaves
8 back bacon rashers
150 ml (¼ pint) dry cider
salt and pepper

Serves **4**
Prep time **10 minutes**
Cooking time **about 10 minutes**

1 Put the flour on a plate and season with salt and pepper. Cut away any tubes from the liver, then dust it with the flour.

2 Heat half the butter with the oil in a frying pan until foaming. Add the sage leaves and cook for about 30 seconds until sizzling. Using a slotted spoon, transfer to a plate lined with kitchen paper.

3 Add the bacon to the pan and fry until golden, then transfer to the plate, cover with foil and keep warm.

4 Add the liver to the pan and fry for about 2 minutes until deep golden. Turn the slices over and return the bacon and sage to the pan. Cook for a further 1-2 minutes until still slightly pink in the middle, or until cooked to your liking. Transfer to a plate, cover with foil and keep warm.

5 Add the cider to the pan and let it bubble until slightly reduced, scraping up any residue. Whisk in the remaining butter and adjust the seasoning if necessary. Serve the liver and bacon with the sauce spooned over and scattered with the sage leaves.

LIVER WITH LEEKS
& *Cannellini Beans*

4 tablespoons plain flour
4 pieces of calves' liver, about
 125 g (4 oz) each
4 teaspoons olive oil
4 large leeks, trimmed and
 sliced
4 lean back bacon rashers,
 chopped
500 g (1 lb) canned cannellini
 beans, drained
4 tablespoons crème fraîche
salt and pepper
chopped parsley or thyme, to
 garnish

Serves **4**
Prep time **10 minutes**
Cooking time **10 minutes**

1 Put the flour on a plate and season with salt and pepper, then coat the liver in the flour.

2 Heat half the oil in a frying pan, add the liver and fry for about 2 minutes on each side until still slightly pink in the middle, or until cooked to your liking. Transfer to a plate, cover with foil and keep warm.

3 Heat the remaining oil in the frying pan, add the leeks and bacon and cook for 3-4 minutes, or until the leeks are softened and the bacon is cooked through. Stir in the cannellini beans and crème fraîche, season with pepper and heat through.

4 Serve the liver with the beans, scattered with chopped parsley or thyme.

Rose-Scented LAMB WITH AUBERGINES

1 Heat 3 tablespoons of the oil in a large saucepan, add the aubergines and cook for about 10 minutes, stirring frequently, until browned. Transfer to a plate.

2 Heat the remaining oil in the pan and fry the lamb in batches until browned, transferring the browned meat to a plate with a slotted spoon. Return all the meat to the pan, add the onions and fry for a further 5 minutes. Add the garlic and spices and fry for a further 2 minutes.

3 Stir in the ginger, tomatoes and stock and bring to a gentle simmer. Cover with a lid or foil and cook for about 1 hour, or until the lamb is tender. Stir in the aubergines, dates and rosewater and cook for a further 20 minutes, stirring occasionally, until the aubergines are tender.

4 Once the lamb is almost ready, put the couscous in a heatproof bowl and pour over 400 ml (14 fl oz) boiling water. Cover with clingfilm and leave to stand for 5 minutes, then fluff up with a fork.

5 Season the lamb with salt and pepper and add a little hot water if necessary. Serve with the couscous.

5 tablespoons olive oil
2 aubergines, diced
1 kg (2 lb) lean shoulder of lamb, excess fat removed and cut into small chunks
2 onions, chopped
3 garlic cloves, chopped
1 teaspoon each of ground turmeric, cinnamon, cumin and coriander
½ teaspoon ground cloves
1.5 cm (½ inch) piece of fresh root ginger, peeled and finely chopped
400 g (13 oz) can chopped tomatoes
300 ml (½ pint) hot lamb or chicken stock
125 g (4 oz) pitted dates, roughly chopped
1 teaspoon rosewater
325 g (11 oz) couscous
salt and pepper

Serves 6
Prep time 20 minutes
Cooking time about 1¾ hours

SAUSAGE &
Sweet Potato Hash

3 tablespoons olive oil
8 pork sausages
3 large red onions, thinly sliced
1 teaspoon caster sugar
500 g (1 lb) sweet potatoes,
　scrubbed and cut into small
　chunks
8 sage leaves
2 tablespoons balsamic vinegar
salt and pepper

Serves **4**
Prep time **15 minutes**
Cooking time **45 minutes**

1 Heat the oil in a frying pan, add the sausages and fry for about 10 minutes, turning frequently, until browned. Transfer to a plate.

2 Add the onions and sugar to the pan and cook gently, stirring frequently, until lightly browned. Return the sausages to the pan with the sweet potatoes, sage leaves and a little salt and pepper.

3 Cover the pan with a lid or foil and cook over a very gentle heat for about 25 minutes, or until the potatoes are tender and the sausages are cooked through. Drizzle with the vinegar and adjust the seasoning if necessary, before serving.

SPICY SAUSAGE
& rocket pasta

2 tablespoons olive oil
8 Italian-style sausages, skins
  removed
400 ml (14 fl oz) passata
1 teaspoon dried chilli flakes
4 handfuls of rocket leaves
salt and pepper

To serve
ready-cooked penne or other
  pasta (see page 10)
grated Parmesan cheese

Serves **4**
Prep time **10 minutes**
Cooking time **15 minutes**

1 Heat the oil in a frying pan, break the sausages into small pieces and add to the pan, then fry for about 5 minutes, turning occasionally, until browned.

2 Add the passata and chilli flakes and season with salt and pepper. Cover with a lid and bring to the boil, then simmer gently for about 5 minutes, or until the sauce is slightly reduced and the sausage meat is cooked through.

3 Add the pasta to the sauce, toss well to coat and heat through. Remove from the heat, stir in the rocket and serve with grated Parmesan.

EASY CASSOULET

2 tablespoons olive oil
4 Cumberland sausages
4 boneless, skinless chicken
  thighs, opened out flat
1 large onion, chopped
2 celery sticks, chopped
2 teaspoons smoked paprika
2 x 400 g (13 oz) cans chopped
  tomatoes with garlic and
  herbs
2 x 400 g (13 oz) cans cannellini
  beans, drained
2 tablespoons chopped parsley
salt and pepper

1 Heat the oil in a large saucepan, add the sausages and chicken thighs and fry for about 5 minutes, turning occasionally, until browned. Remove the meat from the pan and slice the sausages.

2 Add the onion and celery to the pan and fry for 2–3 minutes until slightly softened. Add the paprika, stir well and return the sausages and chicken to the pan.

3 Add the tomatoes and beans and season with salt and pepper. Bring to the boil, then cover with a lid and simmer gently for about 20 minutes, or until the meat is cooked through. Serve sprinkled with the parsley.

Serves **4**
Prep time **15 minutes**
Cooking time **30 minutes**

COOKING TIP

For an authentic cassoulet, fry 8 tablespoons fresh white breadcrumbs in 1 tablespoon olive oil until golden and serve sprinkled over the cooked dish.

CAMPFIRE
PORK GOULASH
with Caraway Dumplings

2 tablespoons vegetable oil
1 kg (2 lb) lean diced pork
2 onions, sliced
1 tablespoon paprika
4 tablespoons tomato purée
750 ml (1¼ pints) hot pork or
  chicken stock
3 tablespoons light muscovado
  sugar
2 tablespoons red wine vinegar
½ red cabbage, shredded
salt and pepper

Dumplings
150 g (5 oz) self-raising flour
75 g (3 oz) beef or vegetable
  suet
1 teaspoon caraway seeds

Serves **6**
Prep time **20 minutes**
Cooking time **1¾-2 hours**

1 Heat a large saucepan. Add the oil and fry the pork in batches until browned, transferring the browned meat to a plate with a slotted spoon. Return all the meat to the pan with the onions and fry, stirring, for 5 minutes.

2 Add the paprika, tomato purée, stock, sugar and vinegar to the pan and bring to a simmer. Cover with a lid and cook very gently for 1-1¼ hours until the meat is very tender, stirring frequently.

3 Add the cabbage to the pan and cook for a further 20 minutes until tender.

4 Meanwhile, mix the flour, suet and caraway seeds in a bowl and season lightly with salt and pepper. Stir in enough cold water to make a thick, sticky paste.

5 Stir a little hot water into the goulash if it has dried out. (It should be really juicy as the dumplings will absorb some of the stock.) Place dessertspoonfuls of the dumpling mixture over the goulash. Cover with the lid and cook for a further 10-15 minutes until the dumplings are light and fluffy.

CHORIZO WITH LENTILS
& *Red Wine*

1 Heat the oil in a frying pan, add the chorizo and fry for 1-2 minutes on each side until golden and the natural oil is released. Transfer to a plate.

2 Add the onion to the pan and cook over a medium heat for about 5 minutes until softened. Stir in the lentils and wine, bring to a simmer and cook for a few minutes.

3 Pour in the stock, return the chorizo to the pan and simmer for about 25 minutes, or until most of the liquid is absorbed and the lentils are tender. Scatter with chopped parsley and serve with plenty of bread.

1 tablespoon olive oil
250 g (8 oz) chorizo sausage, thickly sliced
1 finely chopped onion
150 g (5 oz) Puy lentils
125 ml (4 fl oz) fruity red wine
500 ml (17 fl oz) hot chicken stock
chopped parsley, to garnish
crusty bread, to serve

Serves 4
Prep time **10 minutes**
Cooking time **about 40 minutes**

CHUNKY CHORIZO,
pasta & bean soup

THIS SUBSTANTIAL SOUP IS BASED ON THE ITALIAN CLASSIC, PASTA E FAGIOLI – PASTA AND BEANS, IN ENGLISH.

4 tablespoons olive oil
1 large onion, chopped
50 g (2 oz) chorizo sausage, chopped
4 garlic cloves, crushed
2 tablespoons chopped thyme
1.2 litres (2 pints) passata
750 ml (1¼ pints) hot chicken stock
2 x 400 g (13 oz) cans borlotti beans, drained
200 g (7 oz) small dried pasta shapes (such as conchigliette)
3 tablespoons chopped basil
salt and pepper
grated Parmesan cheese, to serve

Serves 4
Prep time 10 minutes
Cooking time 40 minutes

1 Heat the oil in a saucepan, add the onion, chorizo, garlic and thyme and fry for about 5 minutes, or until the onion is softened and the chorizo is golden.

2 Add the passata, stock, borlotti beans, salt and pepper to the pan. Bring to the boil, then cover with a lid and simmer gently for 20 minutes.

3 Stir in the pasta and basil and cook for a further 8-10 minutes, or until the pasta is tender. Adjust the seasoning if necessary, spoon into bowls and serve topped with grated Parmesan.

CHORIZO HASH
WITH COURGETTES,
POTATOES & EGGS

2 tablespoons olive oil
500 g (1 lb) potatoes, diced
2 red onions, chopped
100 g (3½ oz) chorizo or black
   pudding, cut into small dice
2 courgettes, cut into small dice
10 cherry tomatoes, halved
4 eggs
salt and pepper

Serves **4**
Prep time **20 minutes**
Cooking time **about 45 minutes**

1 Heat the oil in a frying pan, add the potatoes and cook over a medium heat for 15 minutes, or until softened and beginning to colour.

2 Add the onions, sausage and courgettes and cook for a further 15 minutes, stirring frequently, until the ingredients are soft and lightly browned. Stir in the tomatoes and a little salt and pepper.

3 Spread the ingredients in an even layer and make 4 indentations in the mixture. Break an egg into each and continue to cook for 15 minutes, or until the eggs are lightly set.

COOKING TIP

You can speed up the cooking time by covering the pan with a lid or foil, or by spooning the diced ingredients over the eggs once they start to turn opaque.

Fire it up
RISOTTO

1 Heat half the oil in a large saucepan, add the bacon and cook, stirring, until crisp. Transfer to a plate.

2 Add the remaining oil and onion to the pan and cook, stirring, for about 5 minutes, adding the garlic once the onion is softened.

3 Stir the rice into the pan and pour in about 150 ml (¼ pint) of the stock. Cook, stirring, until the stock is absorbed. Pour in a little more stock and cook again, stirring as the rice starts to swell. Continue to add the stock, stirring frequently, until the rice is just tender. If the risotto is too dry, add extra boiling water as necessary.

4 Stir in the bacon, beans and cheese, season with a little salt and pepper and heat through. Stir in the rocket leaves, spinach or nettle tops and serve once they've wilted and the beans are tender.

2 tablespoons olive oil
100 g (3½ oz) thin-cut streaky bacon, chopped
1 large onion, chopped
2 garlic cloves, finely chopped
350 g (11½ oz) risotto rice
1 litre (1¾ pints) hot chicken or vegetable stock (made with 2 stock cubes)
150 g (5 oz) fresh baby broad beans
100 g (3½ oz) Cheddar cheese, grated
handful of rocket leaves, baby spinach leaves or nettle tops
salt and pepper

Serves 4
Prep time **15 minutes**
Cooking time **about 40 minutes**

FIRST AID &
SAFETY

Camping is generally a fairly safe holiday choice but if you go unprepared or aren't aware of the safety risks, you could end up cutting your trip short with a trip to the hospital.

FIRST AID

Always check your first aid kit before you leave home and make sure everyone in your party knows where it's kept. If you take prescription medicine, make sure you have ample supplies to last while you're away and keep a note of the closest medical facilities and pharmacy. The most likely injuries to occur will be stings, insect bites, cuts or sprains so include plenty of plasters, antiseptic cream and sting relief in your first aid kit.

CAMPSITE HAZARDS

Fire is one of the biggest hazards on a campsite, which is why it's so important to choose a safe spot for your campfire – far away from your own and other people's tents, and away from trees and any other combustible materials. Always make sure your campfire is fully extinguished before you leave it (see page 83) and never leave children alone by a campfire.

TRIPS AND FALLS

Tent pegs and guy ropes can be the cause of many a twisted ankle, particularly at night-time, when it's more difficult to see the ropes and to judge distances. When you're walking around the site at night, keep well clear of the tents and always carry a torch to check for any other obstacles that might be blocking your path.

CHILDREN

Camping offers kids a huge amount of freedom but it's important to make them aware of potential dangers as well. Always set limits as to how far they can roam away from the tent and about staying together when they do. Some campsites offer wristbands for kids, which you can write a contact number on, in case they get lost. Another option is a set of walkie-talkies – these could also come in handy for treasure hunts and spy games.

SUN SAFETY

It doesn't have to be blazing sunshine to get sunburnt – in fact, you're more likely to be caught unawares on a cloudy day when you're less fastidious about sun protection. Cover up during the heat of the day and wear sunhats if you're going for a hike or spending a lot of time outdoors.

Chicken
WITH ONION, LEMON & ANCHOVIES

4 tablespoons olive oil
1 lemon, cut into wedges
12 boneless, skinless chicken
  thighs, each cut in half
4 onions, thinly sliced
½ teaspoon caster sugar
2 garlic cloves, chopped
100 ml (3½ fl oz) dry white wine
150 ml (¼ pint) hot chicken
  stock
50 g (2 oz) anchovy fillets,
  chopped
handful of parsley, chopped
salt and pepper

Serves 6
Prep time **20 minutes**
Cooking time **about 1¼ hours**

1 Heat 1 tablespoon of the oil in a large saucepan, add the lemon wedges and brown lightly on the cut sides, then transfer to a plate.

2 Heat another 1 tablespoon of the oil in the pan, add the chicken and brown lightly on all sides. Transfer to a plate.

3 Add the remaining oil to the pan and tip in the onions, add the sugar and fry gently for about 15 minutes, or until the onions are soft and deep golden. Stir in the garlic and cook for a further 1 minute.

4 Return the chicken to the pan with the wine, stock and anchovy fillets and bring to a simmer. Cover with a lid and cook gently for 45 minutes, or until the chicken is tender and cooked through, stirring frequently to stop the base of the pan catching. Season to taste with salt and pepper and stir in the parsley to serve.

PAN-FRIED
CHICKEN LIVERS
WITH FENNEL

1 Put the flour on a plate and season with a little salt and pepper, then coat the chicken livers in the flour.

2 Heat the oil in a frying pan and stir-fry the fennel over a medium-high heat for 3 minutes. Add the liver to the pan and cook for 5-8 minutes, stirring gently, until the liver is cooked to your liking.

3 Slowly stir in the parsley. Pour in the lemon juice, which will make a sizzling sound, then serve with watercress leaves.

1 tablespoon plain flour
225 g (7½ oz) chicken livers, trimmed
2 teaspoons olive oil
225 g (7½ oz) fennel bulb and leaves, trimmed and sliced
3 tablespoons chopped flat leaf parsley
2 tablespoons lemon juice
salt and pepper
watercress leaves, to serve

Serves 4
Prep time **10 minutes**
Cooking time **10-12 minutes**

CHERRY TOMATO & COD STIR-FRY WITH BACON

1 Heat the oil in a frying pan, add the spring onions, garlic and bacon and cook over a high heat for about 3 minutes, stirring frequently, until the onions are softened and the bacon is browned.

2 Add the tomatoes and fish and cook over a medium heat for about 3-4 minutes, or until the fish is opaque and cooked through, stirring gently and tossing occasionally so that the fish cubes stay intact as much as possible.

3 Scatter over the lemon rind and spinach, cover with a lid and cook for about 2 minutes until the spinach has wilted, then gently fold the ingredients together.

4 Scatter over the feta and serve with crusty bread to mop up the juices.

2 tablespoons olive oil
1 bunch of spring onions, trimmed and roughly chopped
1 garlic clove, thinly sliced
175 g (6 oz) rindless streaky bacon, chopped
250 g (8 oz) cherry tomatoes, halved
375 g (12 oz) skinless cod, coley or haddock fillet, cut into cubes
finely grated rind of 1 lemon
2 large handfuls of spinach leaves
150 g (5 oz) feta cheese, crumbled
crusty bread, to serve

Serves **4**
Prep time **15 minutes**
Cooking time **10 minutes**

LEMONY PRAWNS
& broccoli stir-fry

3 tablespoons vegetable oil
1 large red onion, sliced
1 bunch of spring onions, trimmed and roughly chopped
250 g (8 oz) tenderstem broccoli, trimmed and cut into 7 cm (3 inch) lengths
250 g (8 oz) cooked peeled prawns
finely grated rind and juice of 1 lemon
3 tablespoons light soy sauce
175 g (6 oz) ready-to-eat stir-fry rice
salt

Serves 4
Prep time **10 minutes**
Cooking time **15 minutes**

1 Heat the oil in a frying pan, add the onion and cook over a medium-high heat for about 5 minutes, stirring frequently, until softened. Add the spring onions, broccoli and prawns and stir-fry for 4 minutes.

2 Add the lemon rind and juice and soy sauce to the pan and stir well, then add the rice and stir-fry until all the ingredients are piping hot and well mixed. Serve immediately.

Piri Piri Prawns
& BEANS

1 Put the garlic and chillies on a square of heavy-duty foil. Bring the foil up and seal loosely, then tuck between hot coals or logs to cook for about 30 minutes until softened.

2 Mix together the prawns, beans, peppers, oil, vinegar and parsley in a bowl, then spoon the mixture into the centres of four large squares of heavy-duty foil.

3 Carefully remove the garlic and chillies from the foil parcel. Squeeze the garlic from their skins and add a clove and a chilli half to each prawn portion. Season with salt, then bring the foil up around the filling and seal well.

4 Tuck the parcels between hot coals or logs to cook for about 20-40 minutes, or until the prawns turn pink and are cooked through. Rotate the parcels during cooking.

5 Toast the bread on a grill rack over the barbecue or campfire until lightly charred.

6 Carefully open up the parcels, spread the garlic over the toast and pile the prawns and beans on top.

4 garlic cloves, unpeeled
2 red or green chillies, deseeded and halved
300 g (10 oz) raw peeled prawns
400 g (13 oz) can haricot beans, drained
100 g (3½ oz) piquillo peppers from a jar, drained and diced
6 tablespoons olive oil
2 tablespoons sherry vinegar or white wine vinegar
3 tablespoons chopped parsley
salt
baguette or ciabatta slices, to serve

Serves **4**
Prep time **20 minutes**
Cooking time **¾-1¼ hours**

TUNA & OLIVE PASTA

1 Heat the oil in a large saucepan, add the onion and cook over a medium heat for about 5 minutes until softened. Add the garlic and cook for a further 1 minute.

2 Add the chopped tomatoes and chilli flakes, if using, and bring to a simmer, then cook gently for about 10 minutes until thickened slightly.

3 Stir the tuna and olives into the sauce, add the pasta and toss together. Heat through until piping hot.

3 tablespoons olive oil
1 red onion, sliced
2 garlic cloves, chopped
2 x 400 g (13 oz) cans chopped
  tomatoes
½ teaspoon dried chilli flakes
  (optional)
185 g (6½ oz) can tuna in brine
  or oil, drained and flaked
75 g (3 oz) pitted black or green
  olives, roughly chopped
ready-cooked penne or other
  pasta (see page 10), to serve

Serves **4**
Prep time **10 minutes**
Cooking time **20 minutes**

Tuna Fishcakes

2 x 425 g (14 oz) cans tuna in
  olive oil, drained
300 g (10 oz) ricotta cheese
6 spring onions, finely chopped
grated rind and juice of 1 lime
1 tablespoon chopped dill
1 egg, beaten
3 tablespoons olive oil
100 g (3½ oz) salad leaves
salt and pepper

Garlic and herb mayonnaise
1 crushed garlic clove, plus extra
  if required
2 teaspoons lime juice
1 tablespoon chopped fresh
  coriander
pinch of cayenne pepper
150 g (5 oz) good-quality shop-
  bought mayonnaise

Serves 4
Prep time **20 minutes**
Cooking time **20 minutes**

1 Flake the tuna into a bowl and beat in the ricotta, spring onions, lime rind, dill, egg and salt and pepper to taste. Reserve 2 teaspoons of the lime juice and beat the remainder into the tuna mixture. Divide into 12 and shape into small cakes about 7 cm (3 inches) in diameter.

2 Heat 1 tablespoon of the oil in a frying pan, add half the fish cakes and cook over a medium heat for 4–5 minutes on each side until golden and heated through. (Cook for slightly longer over a low heat if they start to over-brown.) Transfer to a plate, cover with foil and keep warm. Repeat with another tablespoon of oil and the remaining fish cakes.

3 Meanwhile, to make the garlic mayonnaise, mix together the garlic, lime juice, coriander, cayenne and mayonnaise in a bowl. Taste and add more garlic, if liked.

4 Whisk together the remaining oil and lime juice in a bowl and toss with the salad leaves. Serve the fish cakes with the salad and mayonnaise.

CREAMY SCALLOPS
WITH LEEKS

1 Melt half the butter in a frying pan and cook the scallops and bacon over a high heat for 2 minutes, stirring frequently, until just golden and cooked through. Transfer to a plate, cover with foil and keep warm.

2 Add the remaining butter to the pan and cook the leeks over a medium heat for about 5 minutes, stirring occasionally, until softened and lightly browned in places. Add the créme fraîche and lemon rind and season well with pepper.

3 Return the scallops to the pan and toss into the creamy leeks. Serve immediately with crusty bread.

4 tablespoons butter
16 shelled and cleaned scallops, halved
1 rindless streaky bacon rasher, roughly snipped
3 leeks, trimmed and sliced
200 ml (7 fl oz) créme fraîche
finely grated rind of 1 lemon
pepper
crusty bread, to serve

Serves 4
Prep time 10 minutes
Cooking time 10 minutes

CAMPING TIP

For scallop kebabs for the barbecue, cut 8 streaky bacon rashers in half and wrap around each scallop. Thread 4 scallops each onto 4 metal kebab skewers and brush with olive oil. Cook for 2–3 minutes on each side until brown.

CAMPFIRE
FISH STEW WITH BASIL & MOZZARELLA TOASTIES

1 Heat half the oil in a large saucepan and fry the shallots until softened. Add the squid and fry until opaque. Transfer to a plate and cover with foil.

2 Add the remaining oil to the pan with the peppers and fry for 10-15 minutes until softened. Stir in the garlic, passata, capers, sugar and stock. Crumble in the saffron and bring to a simmer. Cover with a lid and cook for about 45 minutes, or until the peppers are very tender.

3 Meanwhile, to make the toasties, split the pittas along one edge and spread one side of each cavity with the pesto. Top with the mozzarella slices, basil leaves and a little salt and pepper.

4 Cut the fish into large chunks, discarding any stray bones. Stir into the stew with the squid and shallots and cook for about 5 minutes, or until the fish is cooked through.

5 While the fish is cooking, put the toasties on the grill rack and cook until lightly browned. Alternatively, wrap them individually in foil and tuck between hot coals or logs to heat.

6 Season the stew with salt and pepper and serve with the toasties.

75 ml (3 fl oz) olive oil
6 shallots, finely sliced
8 squid tubes, cut into rings
2 red peppers, cored, deseeded and cut into small chunks
4 garlic cloves, finely chopped
400 g (13 oz) passata
2 tablespoons capers, drained
1 teaspoon caster sugar
500 ml (17 fl oz) hot fish or chicken stock
½ teaspoon saffron strands
1 kg (2 lb) mixed white fish fillets (such as cod, haddock, pollock, monkfish, halibut, bream or mullet fillets), skinned
salt and pepper

Basil and mozzarella toasties
4 pitta breads
2 tablespoons ready-made pesto
125 g (4 oz) mozzarella, thinly sliced
handful of basil leaves, shredded

Serves **4**
Prep time **30 minutes**
Cooking time **about 1¼ hours**

Paella

1 Heat half the oil in a large frying pan (or paella pan), add the prawns and cook until they turn pink and are cooked through. Transfer to a plate. Add the chicken to the pan and fry until golden.

2 Add the remaining oil to the pan with the chorizo, pepper and onion and fry until the onion is soft and the chorizo has turned the oil golden. Tip in the rice and stir to combine, then crumble over the saffron.

3 Pour in the stock and bring to a gentle simmer. Place the pan over an area of the fire that's not too hot and cover with a lid or foil. Leave to cook gently for 20-30 minutes, or until the rice is tender and the chicken is cooked through. Drizzle a little hot water over the rice to stop it drying out, if necessary.

4 Return the prawns to the pan and scatter with the mussels, if using. Re-cover with a lid or foil to trap in the steam and cook for a further few minutes until the mussels have opened up. Discard any mussels that remain closed. Season to taste with salt and pepper and serve with lemon wedges.

100 ml (3½ fl oz) olive oil
8 large raw peeled prawns
4 boneless, skinless chicken thighs, cut into small chunks
125 g (4 oz) chorizo sausage, diced
1 red or green pepper, cored, deseeded and diced
1 onion, chopped
250 g (8 oz) paella rice
large pinch of saffron strands
500 ml (17 fl oz) hot chicken or fish stock
250 g (8 oz) fresh mussels, scrubbed and debearded (optional)
salt and pepper
lemon wedges, to serve

Serves 4
Prep time **20 minutes**
Cooking time **about 40-50 minutes**

SPINACH, RICOTTA
& Basil Penne

1 tablespoon olive oil
1 teaspoon chopped garlic
150 g (5 oz) spinach leaves,
   finely chopped
2 tablespoons chopped basil
250 g (8 oz) ricotta cheese
100 ml (3½ fl oz) dry white wine
salt and pepper

To serve
cooked penne or other pasta
   (see page 10)
Parmesan cheese shavings

Serves **4**
Prep time **5 minutes**
Cooking time **6-8 minutes**

1 Heat the oil in a large saucepan, add the garlic and cook for 2 minutes. Stir in the spinach and cook for 1-2 minutes until wilted. Add the basil, ricotta and wine, season to taste with salt and pepper and cook gently until the ricotta has melted.

2 Stir the pasta into the ricotta mixture, toss well and heat through until piping hot. Serve topped with Parmesan shavings and freshly ground black pepper.

TOMATO, ROSEMARY & CANNELLINI BEAN STEW

1 Heat the oil in a frying pan, add the onion and cook over medium heat for about 5 minutes, stirring occasionally, until softened. Add the garlic purée and rosemary and cook, stirring constantly, for another 30 seconds.

2 Add the beans and tomato sauce and bring to the boil. Cover with a lid and simmer gently for about 7 minutes, or until piping hot. Serve with crusty bread for mopping up the juices.

3 tablespoons olive oil
1 large red onion, sliced
2 teaspoons garlic purée
2 tablespoons chopped
  rosemary leaves
2 x 400 g (13 oz) cans cannellini
  beans, drained
1 x 500 g (1 lb) jar tomato pasta
  sauce
crusty bread, to serve

Serves **4**
Prep time **5 minutes**
Cooking time **15 minutes**

PUY LENTIL *Stew*

1 Heat the oil in a large saucepan, add the peppers, onion, garlic and fennel and cook over a medium-high heat for about 5 minutes, stirring frequently, until softened and lightly browned.

2 Stir in the lentils, stock and wine and bring to the boil, then cover with a lid and simmer gently for about 25 minutes, or until the lentils are tender.

3 Serve the stew hot, with garlic bread for mopping up the juices.

4 tablespoons olive oil
1 red pepper, cored, deseeded and cut into chunks
1 green pepper, cored, deseeded and cut into chunks
1 red onion, roughly chopped
1 garlic clove, sliced
1 fennel bulb, trimmed and sliced
250 g (8 oz) Puy lentils, rinsed
600 ml (1 pint) hot vegetable stock
300 ml (½ pint) red wine
Garlic Bread (see page 206), to serve

Serves 4
Prep time **10 minutes**
Cooking time **35 minutes**

Speedy
KIDNEY BEAN & CORIANDER
Curry

2 teaspoons vegetable oil
1 teaspoon cumin seeds
1 tablespoon tomato purée
2 teaspoons curry powder
1 teaspoon ground turmeric
1 teaspoon ground coriander
1 teaspoon ground cumin
2 teaspoons garam masala
400 g (13 oz) can kidney beans, drained
2 spring onions, sliced
2 tablespoons chopped fresh coriander
salt
mixed salad leaves or warm pitta breads, to serve

1 Heat the oil in a frying pan, add the cumin seeds and let them pop for a few seconds. Stir in the tomato purée, curry powder, ground spices and garam masala and blend well together over a low heat.

2 Mix in the kidney beans, spring onions and chopped coriander and heat through. Add salt to taste and stir in a few tablespoons of hot water if you prefer more sauce. Serve the curry hot with mixed salad leaves or in warm pitta breads.

Serves 4
Prep time **5 minutes**
Cooking time **10 minutes**

SICILIAN SPAGHETTI

2 x 50 g (2 oz) cans anchovy
  fillets in olive oil
2 teaspoons chopped garlic
6 tablespoons chopped flat leaf
  parsley
¼ teaspoon dried chilli flakes
  (optional)
juice of 3 lemons
50 g (2 oz) Parmesan cheese,
  grated
pepper

To serve
ready-cooked spaghetti (see
  page 10)
rocket salad

Serves 4
Prep time **5 minutes**
Cooking time **10 minutes**

1 Drain the olive oil from the anchovies into a frying pan and
  add the garlic. Cook over a medium heat for 1 minute, then
add the anchovies and cook for about 2–3 minutes until the
anchovies begin to soften and break up. Add the parsley and
chilli flakes, if using, then stir in the lemon juice.

2 Add the pasta, season with pepper, toss well and heat
  through until piping hot. Stir in most of the Parmesan,
reserving a little for garnish.

3 Sprinkle the pasta with the reserved Parmesan and serve
  with a rocket salad.

Basil & Tomato Stew

1 Quarter and deseed the tomatoes, scooping out the pulp into a sieve over a bowl to catch the juices.

2 Heat 4 tablespoons of the oil in a large saucepan, add the onions and celery and cook over a medium heat for about 5 minutes until softened. Add the garlic and mushrooms and fry for a further 3 minutes.

3 Add the tomatoes and their juices, sun-dried tomato paste, stock, sugar and capers and bring to the boil, then simmer gently for about 5 minutes.

4 Tear the herbs into pieces, add to the pan with a little salt and pepper and cook for 1 minute. Ladle into bowls, drizzle with the remaining oil and serve with crusty bread.

1 kg (2 lb) ripe tomatoes, skinned
6 tablespoons olive oil
2 onions, chopped
4 celery sticks, sliced
4 plump garlic cloves, thinly sliced
175 g (6 oz) mushrooms, sliced
3 tablespoons sun-dried tomato paste
600 ml (1 pint) vegetable stock
1 tablespoon muscovado sugar
3 tablespoons capers, drained
large handful of basil leaves
large handful of chervil or flat leaf parsley
salt and pepper
crusty bread, to serve

Serves **4**
Prep time **15 minutes**
Cooking time **15 minutes**

CAMPING TIP

Invest in a head torch – it will be the most indispensable piece of equipment on your camping trip (apart from the tent possibly). From after-dark dinner prep to nocturnal calls of nature, the head torch is essential for hands-free activities.

RATATOUILLE

4 tablespoons olive oil
2 large onions, thinly sliced
3 large garlic cloves, crushed
2 large red peppers, cored,
   deseeded and cut into squares
1 large yellow pepper, cored,
   deseeded and cut into squares
2 large aubergines, quartered
   lengthways and cut into 1 cm
   (½ inch) cubes
2 courgettes, cut into 1 cm
   (½ inch) cubes
2 tablespoons tomato purée
400 g (13 oz) can plum
   tomatoes
12 basil leaves, chopped
1 tablespoon finely chopped
   marjoram or oregano
1 teaspoon finely chopped
   thyme
1 tablespoon paprika
2-4 tablespoons finely chopped
   parsley
salt and pepper
crusty bread, to serve

Serves 8
Prep time 15 minutes
Cooking time 35-50 minutes

1 Heat the oil in a large saucepan, add the onions and garlic and cook over a medium heat for about 5-10 minutes until softened but not browned. Add the peppers and cook for a further 5 minutes, then stir in the aubergines and courgettes.

2 Add the tomato purée, plum tomatoes, basil, majoram or oregano, thyme and paprika and season to taste with salt and pepper.

3 Stir to combine and bring to the boil, then cover with a lid and simmer gently for about 20-30 minutes, or until the vegetables are tender and the sauce is thickened.

4 Stir in the parsley and adjust the seasoning if necessary. Serve hot or cold with crusty bread.

Broad Bean, Lemon & PARMESAN RISOTTO

1 Heat the butter and oil in a large saucepan. Add the onion and garlic and fry gently for about 5 minutes until softened. Add the rice and cook for a further 1 minute, stirring.

2 Add the wine and cook, stirring regularly, until the wine is absorbed. Add a little stock and cook, stirring, until almost absorbed. Continue in the same way, gradually adding more stock, until half the stock is used. Stir in the beans.

3 Gradually add the remaining stock until the mixture is thickened and creamy but still retaining a little bite. This will take about 15-20 minutes.

4 Stir in the Parmesan, lemon rind and juice, and season to taste with salt and pepper. Serve with extra Parmesan cheese.

2 tablespoons butter
2 tablespoons olive oil
1 onion, chopped
2 garlic cloves, crushed
400 g (13 oz) risotto rice
150 ml (¼ pint) dry white wine
1.2 litres (2 pints) hot vegetable
   stock
150 g (5 oz) fresh broad beans
50 g (2 oz) Parmesan cheese,
   grated, plus extra to serve
rind and juice of 1 lemon
salt and pepper

Serves 4
Prep time **5 minutes**
Cooking time **20-25 minutes**

Mushroom STROGANOFF

1 tablespoon vegetable oil
1 large onion, thinly sliced
4 celery sticks, thinly sliced
2 garlic cloves, crushed
600 g (1¼ lb) mushrooms, chopped
2 teaspoons smoked paprika
250 ml (8 fl oz) hot vegetable
   stock
150 ml (½ pint) soured cream
pepper

Serves 4
Prep time **10 minutes**
Cooking time **25 minutes**

1 Heat the oil in a frying pan, add the onion, celery and garlic and cook for about 5 minutes until beginning to soften. Add the mushrooms and paprika and cook for a further 5 minutes.

2 Pour in the stock and cook for a further 10 minutes, or until the liquid is reduced by half.

3 Stir in the soured cream and season with pepper to taste. Cook over a medium heat for 5 minutes. Serve immediately.

COCONUT DHAL
with toasted naan fingers

1 tablespoon vegetable oil
1 onion, roughly chopped
2 tablespoons korma curry
   paste
125 g (4 oz) split red lentils,
   rinsed
400 ml (14 fl oz) can coconut
   milk
naan breads, to serve

Serves 4
Prep time 5 minutes
Cooking time 20 minutes

1 Heat the oil in a saucepan, add the onion and cook over a high heat, stirring, for 1 minute, then stir in the curry paste and lentils.

2 Pour in the coconut milk, then fill the can with water and add to the lentils. Bring to the boil, then simmer briskly, uncovered, for about 10 minutes, or until the lentils are tender and the mixture is thick and pulpy.

3 Meanwhile, lightly toast the naan breads on a grill rack over a barbecue or campfire until warm and golden. Cut into fingers and serve alongside the dhal for dipping.

PANEER, PEA & SPINACH *Curry*

2 tablespoons vegetable oil

1 onion, chopped

1 teaspoon chopped garlic

2 teaspoons peeled and chopped fresh root ginger

2 tablespoons medium curry powder

250 g (8 oz) paneer cheese, cut into 1.5 cm (¾ inch) cubes

400 ml (14 fl oz) can coconut milk

250 g (8 oz) fresh peas, shelled

225 g (7½ oz) baby spinach leaves

salt and pepper

naan breads, to serve

1 Heat the oil in a large saucepan, add the onion, garlic and ginger and cook over a medium heat for about 5 minutes until softened. Add the curry powder and cook for 1 minute, then stir in the paneer and stir-fry for a further 1 minute.

2 Pour over the coconut milk, add the peas and bring to a simmer. Cover with a lid and simmer for about 5 minutes, or until the peas are tender.

3 Stir in the spinach and cook for a further 1 minute until wilted. Season to taste with salt and pepper and serve with naan breads.

Serves **4**
Prep time **10 minutes**
Cooking time **15 minutes**

MIXED VEGETABLE
CURRY

1 Heat the oil in a large saucepan, add the onion and cook over a medium heat, stirring occasionally, for about 10 minutes, or until softened and golden. Alternatively, add the cumin seeds and cook, stirring frequently, until they sizzle.

2 Add the vegetables, chilli powder, coriander, turmeric and salt to taste and cook for 2-3 minutes, stirring constantly.

3 Stir in the tomatoes or lemon juice. If a dry vegetable curry is preferred, add only a little water, cover with a lid and cook gently for 10-12 minutes until dry. For a more moist curry, stir in 300 ml (½ pint) water, cover and simmer for 5-6 minutes until the vegetables are tender. Serve with naan breads.

2-3 tablespoons vegetable oil
1 small onion, chopped, or
   2 teaspoons cumin seeds
500 g (1 lb) mixed vegetables
   (such as potatoes, carrots,
   swede and cauliflower, cut into
   chunks or broken into florets,
   green beans left whole and
   peas)
about 1 teaspoon chilli powder
2 teaspoons ground coriander
½ teaspoon ground turmeric
2-3 tomatoes, chopped, or juice
   of 1 lemon
salt
naan breads, to serve

Serves **4**
Prep time **15 minutes**
Cooking time **20-30 minutes**

3 tablespoons olive oil
1 onion, finely chopped
2 celery sticks, thinly sliced
2 garlic cloves, thinly sliced
2 x 425 g (14 oz) cans butter
  beans, drained
4 tablespoons sun-dried tomato
  paste
900 ml (½ pints) hot vegetable
  stock
1 tablespoon chopped rosemary
  or thyme
salt and pepper
Parmesan cheese shavings,
  to serve

Serves 4
Prep time **5 minutes**
Cooking time **20-25 minutes**

BUTTER BEAN & SUN-DRIED TOMATO SOUP

ALTHOUGH IT TAKES ONLY A FEW MINUTES TO
PREPARE, THIS CHUNKY SOUP DISTINCTLY RESEMBLES
A ROBUST ITALIAN MINESTRONE. IT MAKES A WORTHY
MAIN COURSE SERVED WITH PLENTY OF BREAD.

1 Heat the oil in a saucepan, add the onion and fry for about 3 minutes until beginning to soften. Add the celery and garlic and fry for a further 2 minutes.

2 Add the butter beans, sun-dried tomato paste, stock, rosemary or thyme and a little salt and pepper. Bring to the boil, then cover with a lid and simmer gently for 15 minutes. Serve sprinkled with the Parmesan shavings.

BLACK BEAN
& CABBAGE STEW

4 tablespoons olive oil
1 large onion, chopped
1 leek, trimmed and chopped
3 garlic cloves, sliced
1 tablespoon paprika
2 tablespoons chopped
 marjoram or thyme
625 g (1¼ lb) potatoes, cut
 into small chunks
425 g (14 oz) can black beans
 or black-eyed beans, drained
1 litre (1¾ pints) hot vegetable
 stock
175 g (6 oz) cabbage or spring
 greens, shredded
salt and pepper
chunky bread, to serve

Serves 4
Prep time **10 minutes**
Cooking time **25 minutes**

1 Heat the oil in a large saucepan, add the onion and leek and cook over a medium heat for 3 minutes. Add the garlic and paprika and fry for a further 2 minutes until the vegetables are softened.

2 Add the marjoram or thyme, potatoes, beans and stock and bring to the boil. Cover with a lid and simmer gently for about 10 minutes, or until the potatoes have softened but are not mushy.

3 Add the cabbage or spring greens and season to taste with salt and pepper. Simmer for a further 5 minutes. Serve the stew with chunky bread.

HEARTY DHAL, BUTTERNUT
& SPINACH STEW

2 tablespoons vegetable oil
1 large onion, chopped
1 tablespoon medium curry
  paste
1 litre (1¾ pints) hot vegetable
  stock
200 g (7 oz) yellow split peas,
  rinsed
500 g (1 lb) butternut squash,
  deseeded, peeled and cut into
  1.5 cm (¾ inch) chunks
250 g (8 oz) baby spinach
  leaves
salt
warm naan breads or flatbreads,
  to serve

Serves **4**
Prep time **10 minutes**
Cooking time **about 50
minutes**

1 Heat the oil in a large saucepan, add the onion and fry, stirring, for about 5 minutes until softened. Add the curry paste, stock and split peas and bring to a simmer. Cover with a lid and cook gently for 20 minutes, or until the split peas have softened.

2 Stir in the squash and cook for a further 20 minutes, or until the split peas and squash are very tender. Add the spinach, stirring it in until wilted, adding a little hot water if the stew has dried out. Season to taste with a little salt and serve with warm bread.

CANNELLINI BEANS ON TOAST

2 tablespoons vegetable oil
1 onion, chopped
1 celery stick, thinly sliced
1 teaspoon cornflour
425 g (14 oz) can cannellini
  beans, drained
250 g (8 oz) canned chopped
  tomatoes
300 ml (½ pint) hot vegetable
  stock
1 tablespoon coarse-grain
  mustard
1 tablespoon black treacle
1 tablespoon tomato ketchup
1 tablespoon Worcestershire
  sauce
slices of chunky bread
salt and pepper

Serves 2-3
Prep time **5 minutes**
Cooking time **25-30 minutes**

1 Heat the oil in a saucepan, add the onion and celery and fry for about 5 minutes until golden and softened. Blend the cornflour with 2 tablespoons water and add to the pan with the remaining ingredients.

2 Bring to the boil, then simmer, uncovered, for about 20 minutes, stirring frequently, until the mixture is thickened and pulpy.

3 Toast the bread on a grill rack over a barbecue or campfire until lightly charred. Serve the beans on the toast.

COOKING TIP

To add an extra spicy kick to your beans, add a dash of hot pepper sauce to the saucepan 5 minutes before the end of cooking time.

SPANISH
TORTILLA

1 Heat 1 tablespoon of the olive oil in a frying pan, add the onions and garlic and cook over a medium heat for about 5 minutes until golden and softened, then add the cooked potatoes and heat through.

2 Meanwhile, in a large bowl, beat together the eggs and milk. Add the potatoes, onion and garlic to the egg mixture and stir well.

3 Return the pan to the heat and heat the remaining oil. Tip the potato and egg mixture into the pan and cook over a low heat for 7–8 minutes, or until beginning to set. Place an inverted plate over the pan and turn the pan and plate together to tip the tortilla on to the plate. Slide back into the pan and cook until golden and set underneath.

4 Turn out the tortilla on to a plate and leave to cool. Cut into slices and serve warm or cold.

2 tablespoons olive oil
2 onions, sliced
1 garlic clove, crushed
500 g (1 lb) cooked waxy
  potatoes, sliced
6 eggs
50 ml (2 fl oz) milk

Serves 8
Prep time 10 minutes
Cooking time 20-25 minutes

VEGETABLE & TOFU
STIR-FRY

3 tablespoons vegetable oil
300 g (10 oz) firm tofu, cubed
1 onion, sliced
2 carrots, sliced
150 g (5 oz) broccoli, broken
   into small florets and stalks
   sliced
1 red pepper, cored, deseeded
   and sliced
1 large courgette, sliced
150 g (5 oz) sugar snap peas
2 tablespoons soy sauce
2 tablespoons sweet chilli sauce

To serve
chopped red chillies
Thai or ordinary basil leaves

Serves **4**
Prep time **10 minutes**
Cooking time **7 minutes**

1 Heat 1 tablespoon of the oil in a frying pan until starting to smoke, add the tofu and stir-fry over a high heat for 2 minutes until golden. Transfer to a plate with a slotted spoon.

2 Heat the remaining oil in the pan, add the onion and carrots and stir-fry for 1½ minutes. Add the broccoli and red pepper and stir-fry for 1 minute, then add the courgette and sugar snap peas and stir-fry for 1 minute.

3 Combine the soy and chilli sauces and 125 ml (4 fl oz) water, then add to the pan with the tofu. Cook for 1 minute. Serve scattered with chopped red chillies and basil leaves.

Stir-fried VEGETABLE NOODLES

1 Heat the oil in a frying pan, add the spring onions and carrots and stir-fry for 3 minutes. Add the garlic, chilli flakes, mangetout and mushrooms and stir-fry for 2 minutes. Add the Chinese leaves and stir-fry for 1 minute.

2 Add the noodles to the pan with the soy sauce and hoisin sauce. Stir-fry over a gentle heat for about 3–4 minutes, or until heated through. Serve immediately.

4 tablespoons vegetable oil
1 bunch of spring onions, sliced
2 carrots, thinly sliced
2 garlic cloves, crushed
¼ teaspoon dried chilli flakes
125 g (4 oz) mangetout
125 g (4 oz) shiitake mushrooms, halved
3 Chinese leaves, shredded
250 g (8 oz) fresh medium egg noodles
2 tablespoons light soy sauce
3 tablespoons hoisin sauce

Serves **4**
Prep time **10 minutes**
Cooking time **10 minutes**

**LINGUINE WITH SHREDDED
HAM & EGGS**

JAMAICAN SALMON

TUNA QUESADILLA

SWEETCORN FRITTERS

QUICK & EASY

CRISPY LAMB MOROCCAN ROLLS

250 g (8 oz) minced lamb
1 teaspoon ground cinnamon
3 tablespoons pine nuts
2 naan breads, warmed
200 g (7 oz) hummus
2 tablespoons mint leaves
1 Little Gem lettuce, finely
  shredded (optional)

Serves **2**
Prep time **15 minutes**
Cooking time **about 10
minutes**

1 Heat a frying pan until hot, add the minced lamb and fry for about 10 minutes until golden brown, breaking it up with a wooden spoon. Add the cinnamon and pine nuts and cook for a further 1 minute. Remove the lamb from the heat.

2 Place the warm naan breads on a board and, using a rolling pin, firmly roll to flatten.

3 Mix the hummus with half the mint leaves, then spread in a thick layer over the naans. Spoon over the crispy lamb, then scatter over the shredded lettuce, if using, and the remaining mint leaves. Tightly roll up, cut in half and serve, wrapped in foil if liked.

Linguine
WITH SHREDDED HAM & EGGS

THIS RECIPE IS PUT TOGETHER IN MINUTES AND IS CONVENIENTLY ADAPTABLE.
USE OTHER SHREDDED, COOKED MEATS INSTEAD OF THE HAM IF YOU LIKE.

3 tablespoons chopped flat leaf
  parsley
1 tablespoon coarse-grain
  mustard
2 teaspoons lemon juice
good pinch of caster sugar
3 tablespoons olive oil
100 g (3½ oz) thinly sliced ham
2 spring onions
2 eggs
125 g (4 oz) dried linguine
salt and pepper

Serves **2**
Prep time **10 minutes**
Cooking time **10 minutes**

1 Mix together the parsley, mustard, lemon juice, sugar, oil and a little salt and pepper in a bowl and set aside. Roll up the ham and slice it as thinly as possible. Trim the spring onions, cut them lengthways into thin shreds, then cut into 5 cm (2 inch) lengths.

2 Put the eggs in a small saucepan and just cover with cold water. Bring to the boil and cook for 4 minutes (once the water boils the eggs will usually start to move around).

3 Meanwhile, cook the pasta in a saucepan of salted water for 6–8 minutes, or until just tender. Add the spring onions and cook for a further 30 seconds.

4 Drain the pasta and return to the pan. Stir in the ham and the mustard dressing and pile on to plates. Shell and halve the eggs and serve on top.

Meatballs,
PEAS & PASTA

1 Cut the sausage meat into small pieces and roll into walnut-sized meatballs. Heat half the oil in a frying pan, add the meatballs and cook over a medium heat, stirring frequently, for about 10 minutes, or until cooked through. Transfer to a plate, cover with foil and keep warm.

2 Meanwhile, cook the pasta in a large saucepan of lightly salted boiling water for 6 minutes. Add the peas, return to the boil and cook for a further 4 minutes, or until the peas and pasta are just tender. Drain well, reserving 4 tablespoons of the cooking water, then return to the pan.

3 Add the garlic, sage, chilli flakes and salt and pepper to taste to the meatball pan and cook over a low heat for 2–3 minutes until the garlic is soft but not browned. Stir in the meatballs.

4 Tip the meatball mixture, reserved cooking water and remaining oil into the pasta pan and heat through. Serve topped with grated Parmesan.

500 g (1 lb) beef or pork
  sausages, skins removed
4 tablespoons olive oil
400 g (13 oz) dried fusilli
250 g (8 oz) fresh peas,
  shelled
2 garlic cloves, sliced
2 tablespoons chopped sage
½ teaspoon dried chilli flakes
salt and pepper
grated Parmesan cheese,
  to serve

Serves 4
Prep time 20 minutes
Cooking time 15 minutes

Pappardelle WITH
FIGS, GORGONZOLA & PARMA HAM

THIS RECIPE COMBINES SWEET AND SALTY FLAVOURS, TOSSED IN A
HONEY AND ORANGE DRESSING AND MAKES A GREAT LIGHT LUNCH.

1 Cook the pasta in a large saucepan of salted boiling water
for 2-3 minutes for fresh and 8-10 minutes for dried.

2 Meanwhile, whisk together the honey, mustard, orange
and lemon juice, oil and a little salt and pepper in a bowl.

3 Drain the pasta and return it to the saucepan. Gently mix
in the figs, ham and Gorgonzola. Serve with the dressing
spooned over.

200 g (7 oz) fresh or dried
   pappardelle
2 tablespoons clear honey
2 teaspoons coarse-grain
   mustard
3 tablespoons orange juice
squeeze of lemon juice
3 tablespoons olive oil
4 ripe, juicy figs, cut into thin
   wedges
100 g (3½ oz) Parma ham,
   torn into small pieces
150 g (5 oz) Gorgonzola cheese,
   roughly diced
salt and pepper

Serves **4**
Prep time **10 minutes**
Cooking time **about 2-10
minutes**

CHEESY TURKEY
& Cranberry Melt

4 flat rolls
2 tablespoons wholegrain
  mustard
2 tablespoons cranberry sauce
200 g (7 oz) cooked turkey
  breast, sliced
125 g (4 oz) Cheddar cheese,
  grated

Serves 4
Prep time **5 minutes**
Cooking time **16 minutes**

1 Split the rolls and spread half with the mustard and the other half with the cranberry sauce. Top with the turkey slices and cheese and sandwich together.

2 Heat a dry frying pan until hot, add 2 sandwiches and cook over a medium-high heat for 4 minutes on each side until golden and the cheese has melted. Serve hot.

3 Repeat with the remaining 2 sandwiches.

JAMAICAN SPICED
Salmon with Corn & Okra

4 skinless salmon fillets, about
175 g (6 oz) each
1 tablespoon Jamaican jerk
seasoning
4 corn on the cobs, halved
3 tablespoons olive oil
1 red onion, sliced
250 g (8 oz) okra, trimmed
4 tablespoons butter
½ teaspoon paprika
½ teaspoon ground nutmeg
salt

Serves **4**
Prep time **10 minutes**
Cooking time **15 minutes**

1 Rub each of the salmon fillets with the Jamaican jerk seasoning and set aside.

2 Cook the corn in a large saucepan of boiling water and for about 5 minutes, or until tender. Drain well.

3 Heat 2 tablespoons of the oil in a large saucepan, add the onion and cook over a medium heat, stirring frequently, for 2 minutes. Add the okra and cook, stirring frequently, for about a further 4 minutes until beginning to soften. Add the corn on the cobs to the pan with the butter and spices and toss for a further 2-3 minutes until lightly browned in places.

4 Meanwhile, heat the remaining tablespoon of oil in a frying pan and cook the salmon fillets, spice side down, over a medium heat for 3-4 minutes, then turn over and cook for a further 2 minutes, or until cooked through. Serve hot with the corn and okra mixture.

TUNA QUESADILLA
with Salsa

2 soft flour tortillas
4 tablespoons ready-made
  fresh tomato salsa
2 spring onions, roughly
  chopped
75 g (3 oz) canned tuna,
  drained
50 g (2 oz) canned sweetcorn
  with peppers, drained
75 g (3 oz) mozzarella cheese,
  grated
olive oil, for brushing

Serves **2**
Prep time **5 minutes**
Cooking time **4-6 minutes**

1 Place 1 tortilla on a plate and spread with the salsa. Sprinkle with the spring onions, tuna, sweetcorn and cheese. Place the second tortilla on top and press down.

2 Heat a frying pan and brush with oil. Place the quesadilla in the pan and cook over a medium heat for 2-3 minutes, pressing down with a spatula until the cheese starts to melt.

3 Place an inverted plate over the pan and turn the pan and plate together to tip the quesadilla on to the plate. Slide back into the pan and cook for 2-3 minutes on the other side. Serve cut into wedges.

Pesto &
SALMON PASTA

1 Cook the pasta in a large saucepan of lightly salted boiling water for about 8 minutes, or until almost tender.

2 Meanwhile, heat the oil in a frying pan, add the onion and cook over a medium heat for about 5 minutes until softened.

3 Drain the salmon and discard skin and bones. Flake the flesh.

4 Add the peas to the pasta and cook for a further 5 minutes until just tender. Drain the pasta and peas, retaining a few tablespoons of the cooking water, and return to the pan.

5 Stir in the pesto, lemon juice, Parmesan, onion, reserved water and flaked salmon. Season lightly with salt and pepper and toss gently. Serve with extra Parmesan and a leafy salad.

325 g (11 oz) dried penne
2 tablespoons olive oil
1 onion, thinly sliced
400 g (13 oz) canned salmon
150 g (5 oz) fresh peas, shelled
2 tablespoons ready-made pesto
1 tablespoon lemon juice
25 g (1 oz) Parmesan cheese, grated, plus extra to serve
salt and pepper
leafy salad, to serve

Serves 4
Prep time 10 minutes
Cooking time 15 minutes

PASTA SALAD WITH CRAB,
LIME & ROCKET

IF YOU MAKE THIS BEFORE YOU GO CAMPING, CONTINUE TO THE END OF STEP 2, THEN PACK THE PASTA IN AN AIRTIGHT CONTAINER OR SEALABLE FREEZER BAG AND STORE IN A COOL BOX. ADD THE TOMATOES AND ROCKET JUST BEFORE YOU'RE READY TO EAT.

50 g (2 oz) dried pasta (such as rigatoni)
grated rind and juice of ½ a lime
2 tablespoons crème fraîche
85 g (3¼ oz) canned crab meat, drained
8 cherry tomatoes, halved
handful of rocket leaves

Serves 1
Prep time **5 minutes, plus cooling**
Cooking time **10 minutes**

1 Cook the pasta in a saucepan of boiling water for about 10 minutes, or until tender, then drain and leave to cool.

2 Mix together the lime rind and juice, crème fraîche and crab meat in a large bowl. Add the pasta and mix again.

3 Add the tomatoes and rocket to the bowl, toss everything together and serve.

CAMPING TIP

Buy yourself a cheap groundsheet or tarpaulin and fold it to the same size as your tent. Peg your tent out over the groundsheet; when you pack up, the bottom of your tent will be clean and mud-free. You can clean the groundsheet more easily than the tent.

PRAWN, MANGO & AVOCADO *Wrap*

1 Mix together the crème fraîche and ketchup. Add a few drops of Tabasco sauce to taste. Add the prawns, mango and avocado and toss the mixture together.

2 Divide the mixture among the tortillas, add some watercress, then roll up and serve.

2 tablespoons crème fraîche
2 teaspoons tomato ketchup
few drops of Tabasco sauce
300 g (10 oz) cooked peeled prawns
1 mango, peeled, stoned and thinly sliced
1 avocado, peeled, stoned and sliced
100 g (3½ oz) watercress
4 flour tortillas

Serves 4
Prep time 10 minutes

GRIDDLED *Greek-Style* SANDWICHES

¼ small red onion, thinly sliced
8 cherry tomatoes, quartered
4 pitted black olives, chopped
5 cm (2 inch) piece of cucumber, deseeded and cut into small pieces
1 teaspoon dried oregano
50 g (2 oz) feta cheese, crumbled
1 teaspoon lemon juice
2 round seeded pitta breads
25 g (1 oz) Cheddar cheese, grated
olive oil, for brushing
pepper

Serves **2**
Prep time **15 minutes**
Cooking time **4-6 minutes**

1 Mix together the onion, tomatoes, olives, cucumber, oregano and feta in a small bowl. Add the lemon juice, season to taste with pepper and mix gently.

2 Split each pitta bread in half horizontally. Divide the feta mixture between the bottom halves of the pitta breads, then add the Cheddar. Cover with the top halves of the pitta breads.

3 Brush a griddle pan or frying pan with oil and heat over a medium heat. When hot, add the sandwiches, press down gently with a spatula and cook for about 2-3 minutes on each side, or until golden and the cheese has melted. Serve immediately.

MEDITERRANEAN
Goats' Cheese
OMELETTES

50 ml (2 fl oz) olive oil
500 g (1 lb) cherry tomatoes,
 halved
a little chopped basil
12 eggs
2 tablespoons wholegrain
 mustard
4 tablespoons butter
125 g (4 oz) soft goats' cheese,
 diced
salt and pepper

Serves 4
Prep time **15 minutes**
Cooking time **20-25 minutes**

1 Heat the oil in a frying pan, add the tomatoes and fry for 2-3 minutes until they have softened - if necessary, do this in two batches. Add the basil and season with salt and pepper, then transfer to a bowl, cover with foil and keep warm.

2 Beat the eggs with the mustard in a bowl and season with salt and pepper. Melt a quarter of the butter in a frying pan, then swirl in a quarter of the egg mixture. Fork over the omelette so that it cooks evenly.

3 As soon as it is set on the bottom (but still a little runny in the middle), dot over a quarter of the goats' cheese and cook for a further 30 seconds. Carefully slide the omelette on to a plate, folding it in half as you do so, and serve with a quarter of the tomatoes.

4 Repeat with the remaining mixture to make 3 more omelettes, and serve with the remaining tomatoes.

Caramelized Onion & CHEESE CRÊPES

150 g (5 oz) wholemeal flour
pinch of salt
1 egg, lightly beaten
300 ml (½ pint) milk
1 tablespoon mustard
vegetable oil, for frying

Filling
3 tablespoons butter
3 onions, thinly sliced
2 teaspoons caster sugar
a few thyme sprigs
250 g (8 oz) Emmental or
   Gruyère cheese, grated
salt and pepper

Serves 4
Prep time **10 minutes**
Cooking time **20-30 minutes**

1 Put the flour and salt in a bowl and make a well in the centre. Pour the egg and some of the milk into the well, then beat, gradually incorporating the flour to make a smooth paste. Beat in the remaining milk and the mustard. Set aside.

2 To make the filling, melt the butter in a saucepan, add the onions and sugar and cook over a low heat for about 10-15 minutes, or until they are softened, deep golden and caramelized. Tear the thyme leaves off the stems and add them to the pan with salt and plenty of pepper. Remove from the heat and keep warm.

3 Heat a little oil in a frying pan until it starts to smoke, then pour off the excess into a cup. Pour a quarter of the batter into the pan, tilting it until the bottom is coated with a thin layer. Cook for 1-2 minutes, or until golden underneath. Carefully flip the crêpe over and cook for a further 30-45 seconds until it is golden on the other side.

4 Add a quarter of the onions and cheese to one half of the crêpe and heat briefly until the cheese begins to melt, then flip over and slide on to a plate. Serve immediately.

5 Repeat with the remaining batter and filling to make 3 more crêpes, adding a little more oil to the pan as required.

EGG & MANCHEGO TORTILLAS

1 Beat the eggs with a fork in a bowl, then stir in the onion, chilli and sweetcorn. Season well with salt and pepper.

2 Melt the butter in a large saucepan until foaming, add the egg mixture and cook over a medium heat, stirring constantly, until the eggs are softly scrambled. Immediately remove the pan from the heat and stir in the crumbled Manchego and coriander.

3 Spoon on to the warm tortillas, scatter with green chilli slices, fresh coriander and chives and top with shavings of Manchego. Serve with sweet chilli sauce.

10 eggs
1 onion, finely chopped
1 green chilli, deseeded and
   finely chopped
4 tablespoons canned
   sweetcorn
2 tablespoons butter
75 g (3 oz) Manchego cheese,
   crumbled
1 tablespoon chopped fresh
   coriander
8 flour tortillas, warmed
salt and pepper

To serve
green chilli slices
fresh coriander leaves
snipped chives
Manchego shavings
4 tablespoons sweet chilli sauce

Serves **4**
Prep time **15 minutes**
Cooking time **about 5 minutes**

RICE NOODLES WITH
Green Beans & Ginger

100 g (3½ oz) fine rice noodles
125 g (4 oz) green beans, halved
finely grated rind and juice of 2
limes
1 Thai chilli, deseeded and finely
chopped
2.5 cm (1 inch) piece of fresh
root ginger, peeled and finely
chopped
2 teaspoons caster sugar
small handful of fresh coriander,
chopped
50 g (2 oz) dried pineapple
pieces, chopped

1 Place the noodles in a heatproof bowl, cover with plenty of boiling water and leave to stand for 4 minutes until soft.

2 Meanwhile, cook the beans in a saucepan of boiling water for about 3 minutes, or until tender. Drain.

3 Mix together the lime rind and juice, chilli, ginger, caster sugar and coriander in a small bowl.

4 Drain the noodles and place in a large bowl. Add the cooked beans, pineapple and dressing and toss together lightly before serving.

Serves **4**
Prep time **10 minutes**
Cooking time **5 minutes**

CAMPING TIP

A double-handled wok is a great addition to your camping kit — you can use it as a makeshift washing up bowl, or to carry things about.

RICE NOODLE PANCAKES
with Stir-Fried Vegetables

1 Cook the noodles in a saucepan of lightly salted boiling water for about 3 minutes, or until tender. Drain well. Transfer to a bowl, then add the chilli, ginger, coriander, flour and the 2 teaspoons of oil and mix well. Set aside.

2 Thinly slice the broccoli stalks and cut the florets into small pieces. Cook the stalks in boiling water for 30 seconds, add the florets and cook for a further 30 seconds. Drain the broccoli well.

3 Heat the 2 tablespoons vegetable oil in a frying pan over a high heat, add the onion and stir-fry for 2 minutes. Add the peppers and stir-fry for 3 minutes, or until just softened. Stir in the cooked broccoli, sugar snap peas, hoisin sauce and lime juice and season to taste with salt and pepper. Tip into a bowl, cover with foil and keep warm.

4 Heat some oil in the frying pan to a depth of 1 cm (½ inch). Place 4 large separate spoonfuls of the noodles (half the mixture) in the oil. Fry for about 5 minutes until crisp and lightly coloured. Drain the pancakes on kitchen paper and keep warm. Repeat with the remaining noodle mixture.

5 Reheat the vegetables for 1 minute, if necessary, then pile on to the noodle pancakes and serve.

175 g (6 oz) dried wide rice noodles
1 green chilli, deseeded and sliced
2.5 cm (1 inch) piece of fresh root ginger, peeled and grated
3 tablespoons chopped fresh coriander
2 teaspoons plain flour
2 teaspoons vegetable oil, plus extra for shallow-frying

Stir-fried vegetables
125 g (4 oz) broccoli
2 tablespoons vegetable oil
1 small onion, sliced
1 red pepper, cored, deseeded and sliced
1 yellow or orange pepper, cored, deseeded and sliced
125 g (4 oz) sugar snap peas, halved lengthways
6 tablespoons hoisin sauce
1 tablespoon lime juice
salt and pepper

Serves 4
Prep time **15 minutes**
Cooking time **20 minutes**

SWEETCORN FRITTERS WITH SWEET CHILLI DIP

250 g (8 oz) plain flour
2 eggs
125 ml (4 fl oz) milk
6 spring onions, chopped
2 x 325 g (11 oz) cans sweetcorn,
    drained well
2 tablespoons vegetable oil,
    plus extra if required
salt and pepper
fresh coriander leaves, to
    garnish

Sweet chilli dip
250 g (8 oz) light soft cheese
2 tablespoons sweet chilli sauce

Serves 4
Prep time **10 minutes**
Cooking time **20 minutes**

1 Place the flour in a bowl and make a well in the centre. Break the eggs into the well and add the milk. Gradually whisk the flour into the eggs and milk to make a smooth, thick batter. Stir in the spring onions and sweetcorn and season with salt and pepper.

2 To make the dip, put the soft cheese in a bowl and stir to soften, then lightly stir through the sweet chilli sauce to form a marbled effect.

3 Heat the oil in a frying pan, add spoonfuls of the batter, about 4 at a time, and cook for 2 minutes on each side, or until golden, firm to the touch and heated through. Serve the fritters warm with the dip, sprinkled with coriander leaves.

4 Repeat with the remaining batter, adding extra oil if necessary.

LEMON, RICOTTA
& COURGETTE RIBBON
stir-fry

250 g (8 oz) dried parpardelle
  or tagliatelle
400 g (13 oz) small baby
  courgettes
salt and pepper
green salad, to serve

Lemony ricotta
1 teaspoon fennel seeds
¼ teaspoon dried chilli flakes
  (optional)
12-15 black peppercorns
250 g (8 oz) ricotta cheese
¼ teaspoon ground nutmeg
finely grated rind and juice of 1
  lemon

Serves **4**
Prep time **15 minutes**
Cooking time **about 7
minutes**

1 To make the lemony ricotta, lightly crush the fennel seeds with the chilli flakes, if using, and black peppercorns, then tip into a bowl. Add the ricotta, nutmeg and lemon rind and juice and mix well, then set aside.

2 Cook the pasta in a saucepan of boiling water for about 5 minutes, or until just tender.

3 Meanwhile, slice the courgettes thinly into ribbons using a sharp vegetable peeler.

4 Add the courgettes to the pasta and cook for a further 2 minutes, or until the pasta is tender and the courgettes softened.

5 Drain the pasta and courgettes, reserving 2-3 tablespoons of the cooking liquid. Return the pasta, courgettes and reserved water to the pan, add the lemony ricotta and stir gently to combine. Season with salt and pepper, then serve with a green salad.

ENTERTAINMENT

Camping offers the ideal opportunity to enjoy some good, old-fashioned family entertainment. And let's face it, with everyone gathered together in a relatively small space, devoid of television and other modern media, you're going to need to get creative and plan activities to keep the kids amused during the day and to while away the evenings.

Daytime Activities

NATURE TRAIL

This can be as low-key or high-tech as you want. If you have the time, inclination and knowledge of wildlife, you could prepare sheets of plants and animals to spot. Or, you can simply bundle the kids out of the tent and into the woods and see what you can find. Either way, you'll all get a good dose of fresh air and exercise and build up an appetite for dinner.

SPORTS DAY

Bring a skipping rope, football, tennis balls, Hula Hoops or anything else that doesn't take up too much space in the car but can be easily adapted to set up an impromptu sports day on a sunny afternoon. Running races, wheelbarrow races, dribbling competitions, catching, balancing, jumping and skipping can all be incorporated.

HIDE AND SEEK

No equipment is required for this game that will have the kids squealing in delight.

TREASURE HUNT

No explanation necessary!

Wet Weather Games

CARDS

Bring a couple of packs of cards. If you don't know many games, look some up online before you travel so you have something new for the family to play on rainy days.

BOARD GAMES

It's always good to have a couple of favourite board games tucked away in the car in case the weather turns against you.

PAPER AND PENS

From diaries to drawings, hangman to noughts and crosses, a selection of notepads, pencils and crayons are essential.

Around the Campfire

SCARY STORYTELLING

Before the trip, ask everyone to find a scary story that they can read out around the campfire. You can either designate an evening as 'fright night' or pick someone different to tell their tale each night.

SONG TIME

A campfire isn't a campfire without some rusty guitar playing and drunken sing-alongs. If one of your party plays an instrument it should be obligatory for them to bring it on the trip. If you're travelling with kids, involve them by asking them to choose songs, or letting them put on a performance of their own.

CHARADES

This classic camping game will keep everyone entertained, especially after a couple of drinks.

CURRIED
Cauliflower,
LENTIL & RICE

2 tablespoons vegetable oil
1 large onion, sliced
2 teaspoons cumin seeds
2 tablespoons Jalfrezi curry
   paste
350 g (11½ oz) cauliflower, cut
   into florets
100 g (3½ oz) red lentils, rinsed
150 g (5 oz) basmati rice
700 ml (1¼ pints) hot vegetable
   stock
2 carrots, coarsely grated
50 g (2 oz) toasted cashew nuts
2 handfuls of fresh coriander
   leaves, to garnish

Serves **4**
Prep time **10 minutes**
Cooking time **30 minutes**

1 Heat the oil in a frying pan, add the onion and cook over a medium heat for about 5 minutes until softened. Add the cumin seeds and cook for 30 seconds, then add the curry paste and cook for a further 30 seconds.

2 Add the cauliflower, red lentils, rice and stock and bring to the boil, then cover with a lid and simmer gently for 10-15 minutes, or until cooked through and the liquid is absorbed.

3 Stir in the grated carrots and cook for 2 minutes, adding a little hot water if the mixture is too dry. Sprinkle over the cashews and serve scattered with coriander leaves.

BIG MAC 'N' CHEESE

250 g (8 oz) macaroni
pinch of ground nutmeg
4 tablespoons butter
30 g (1 oz) plain flour
600 ml (1 pint) milk
2 teaspoons Dijon mustard
200 g (7 oz) grated Cheddar
  cheese
4 small tomatoes, cut into
  wedges
salt and pepper

Serves 4
Prep time **10 minutes**
Cooking time **20 minutes**

1 Cook the macaroni in a large saucepan of boiling water for 10-12 minutes, or until tender.

2 Drain the pasta. Dry the saucepan, then add the butter and heat until melted. Stir in the flour, then gradually add the milk and bring to the boil, stirring constantly, until thickened.

3 Stir in the mustard, cheese and plenty of salt and pepper and heat until the cheese has melted. Stir in the macaroni and tomatoes and heat through.

CAMPING TIP

To keep your coolbox as cold
as possible if there are no fridges
or freezers at the campsite, freeze
whatever food you won't be eating on the
first day and pack at the bottom of your
coolbox to de-frost slowly and keep
the box cold.

GREEN CHEESE PASTA

1. Cook the pasta shapes for 8-10 minutes in a saucepan of boiling water, or until just tender. Drain and set aside.

2. Meanwhile, rinse the spinach with water and roughly drain, then cook in a hot frying pan for about 2 minutes until just wilted. Press out any water and chop finely, then return to the pan and toss with the nutmeg. Set aside.

3. Melt the butter in a saucepan. Remove from the heat, add the flour and stir to form a thick paste. Return to the heat and cook gently for a few seconds, stirring constantly. Remove from the heat and gradually add the milk, stirring well after each addition. Return to the heat and bring to the boil, stirring constantly until the sauce has boiled and thickened.

4. Add the spinach, cheese and pasta, stir well to coat and heat through gently.

250 g (8 oz) dried pasta shapes
300 g (10 oz) spinach leaves
1 teaspoon ground nutmeg
4 tablespoons butter
50 g (2 oz) plain flour
600 ml (1 pint) milk
100 g (4 oz) Cheddar cheese, grated

Serves 4
Prep time **10 minutes**
Cooking time **15-20 minutes**

Refried Bean
QUESADILLA

200 g (7 oz) canned refried beans
2 spring onions, chopped
50 g (2 oz) canned sweetcorn, drained
1 tablespoon chopped fresh coriander
2 soft corn tortillas
3 tablespoons ready-made fresh tomato salsa, plus extra to serve
50 g (2 oz) Cheddar or Monterey Jack cheese, grated
olive oil, for brushing

Serves 2
Prep time 5 minutes
Cooking time about 4-6 minutes

1 Mix together the refried beans, spring onions, sweetcorn and coriander in a bowl.

2 Spread 1 tortilla with the bean mixture, top with the salsa and sprinkle over the cheese. Cover with the remaining tortilla.

3 Brush a frying pan or griddle pan with oil and heat over a medium heat. When hot, add the quesadilla and cook over a medium heat for 2-3 minutes, pressing down with a spatula, until the cheese starts to melt.

4 Place a large plate over the pan and turn the quesadilla over on to the plate. Return to the pan and cook for 2-3 minutes on the other side. Cut into wedges and serve with extra tomato salsa.

ORZO RISOTTO
WITH PANCETTA & PEAS

900 ml (1½ pints) hot chicken
  or vegetable stock
350 g (11½ oz) orzo pasta
a knob of butter
1 teaspoon chopped garlic
150 g (5 oz) diced pancetta
200 g (7 oz) fresh peas, shelled
handful of parsley, chopped
75 g (3 oz) Parmesan cheese,
  grated
salt and pepper

Serves 4
Prep time 5
Cooking time 10-15 minutes

1 Place the stock in a saucepan, bring to the boil and add
the pasta.

2 Meanwhile, melt the butter in a small frying pan until
foaming, add the garlic and pancetta and fry for 2 minutes,
or until the pancetta is crispy.

3 Add the pancetta and garlic to the orzo with the peas and
continue to cook over a medium heat for about 7 minutes,
or until the pasta and peas are just tender, stirring occasionally
to prevent the pasta sticking and adding a little more water
if necessary.

4 Season to taste with salt and pepper and stir in the parsley
and most of the Parmesan. Serve immediately, sprinkled
with the remaining Parmesan and freshly ground black pepper.

SIDES, SALADS, SAUCES & SNACKS

180 SARDINES ON RYE

181 SPICED MACKEREL FILLETS

182 EGGS FLORENTINE

184 SMOKED MACKEREL PASTA SALAD

185 SEARED TUNA WITH BEAN & ROCKET SALAD

186 HERBED LAMB WITH FIG SALAD

188 CYPRIOT CHICKEN & HALOUMI SALAD

189 CHICKPEA & HERB SALAD

190 ORANGE & AVOCADO SALAD

192 RIBBONED CARROT SALAD

193 GRIDDLED HALOUMI WITH WARM COUSCOUS SALAD

194 EGG, BASIL & CHEESE SALAD WITH CHERRY TOMATOES

195 SPICY SWEET POTATO & FETA SALAD

196 REAL GUACAMOLE WITH RAW VEGETABLES

198 WARM COURGETTE & LIME SALAD

199 BEER FLATBREADS WITH CHEESE & ONIONS

200 CORN FLATBREADS WITH SWEETCORN & GRUYÈRE

201 BALSAMIC BRAISED LEEKS & PEPPERS

202 MUSTARD & THYME SWEET POTATOES

203 FIRE-BAKED NEW POTATOES WITH GREEN DRESSING

204 BALSAMIC-ROASTED TOMATOES

204 ROASTED RED ONIONS

205 PANZANELLA

206 CRUSHED MINTED PEAS

206 GARLIC BREAD

207 DEVILLED MUSHROOMS

208 TABBOULEH WITH FRUIT & NUTS

210 GREEN COUSCOUS WITH SPICED FRUIT SAUCE

GRIDDLED HALOUMI & WARM
COUSCOUS SALAD

PANZANELLA

REAL GUACAMOLE

Sardines ON RYE

250 g (8 oz) can sardines in oil, drained
125 g (4 oz) cream cheese
2 tablespoons grated cucumber, drained
1 spring onion, finely chopped
6 thin slices of rye bread
butter, for spreading
lettuce leaves

Serves **3**
Prep time **10 minutes**

1 Put the sardines and cream cheese in a bowl and mash together. Stir in the cucumber and spring onion.

2 Spread 3 slices of the rye bread with the butter, add the sardine mixture and lettuce and top with the remaining slices of bread.

CAMPING TIP

If you know you'll be arriving on site fairly late, bring a pre-prepared meal that can be simply heated and served on the first night — setting up camp always takes longer than you think and you'll be tired and hungry by the time the tent is erected.

SPICED
Mackerel Fillets

1 Mix together the oil, paprika and cayenne in a bowl and season to taste with salt and pepper. Make 3 shallow cuts in the skin of each mackerel fillet and brush all over with the spiced oil.

2 Cook the lime quarters and mackerel fillets on a grill rack over a hot barbecue or campfire, skin side down, for about 5 minutes, or until the skin is crispy and the limes are charred. Turn the fish over and cook for a further 1 minute, or until cooked through. Serve with a rocket salad.

2 tablespoons olive oil
1 tablespoon smoked paprika
1 teaspoon cayenne pepper
8 fresh mackerel fillets
2 limes, quartered
salt and pepper
rocket salad, to serve

Serves **4**
Prep time **5 minutes**
Cooking time **6 minutes**

EGGS Florentine

a knob of butter, plus extra for
 spreading
200 g (7 oz) spinach leaves
4 muffins
3 tablespoons chopped parsley
200 ml (7 fl oz) jar hollandaise
 sauce
salt and pepper
4 eggs
1 tablespoon vinegar

Serves 4
Prep time **10 minutes**
Cooking time **10 minutes**

1 Melt the butter in a large saucepan, add the spinach and
 cook over a medium heat, stirring, for 1–2 minutes until
wilted. Season with salt and pepper, cover with a lid and
keep warm.

2 Split the muffins and toast, cut side down, in a griddle pan
 or over a barbecue or campfire until lightly charred. Wrap
in a clean tea towel and keep warm. Mix the parsley and
hollandaise sauce together in a bowl.

3 Meanwhile, bring a large saucepan of water to the boil.
 Break 1 of the eggs into a cup, making sure not to break the
yolk. Add the vinegar to the boiling water, then stir the water
rapidly in a circular motion to make a whirlpool. Carefully slide
the egg into the centre of the pan while the water is still
swirling, holding the cup as close to the water as you can. Cook
for 1–2 minutes, or until the white is firm and the yolk is soft,
then lift out with a slotted spoon.

4 Butter 2 halves of a muffin, then add a quarter of the
 spinach and top with an egg. Spoon over the hollandaise
sauce and serve with freshly ground black pepper.

5 Cook and serve the other 3 eggs in the same way, swirling
 the boiling water into a whirlpool each time before sliding
in the egg.

SMOKED MACKEREL
PASTA SALAD

1 Cook the pasta in a large saucepan of lightly salted boiling water for about 10-12 minutes, or until just tender. Drain and leave to cool.

2 Meanwhile, cook the beans in a saucepan of lightly salted boiling water for about 5 minutes, or until just tender. Drain and leave to cool.

3 To make the dressing, mix together all the ingredients in a small bowl and season with salt and pepper.

4 Tip the pasta into a large bowl, then flake the smoked mackerel fillets into the bowl. Add the salad leaves, cucumber, spring onions and cooled beans, then toss with some of the dressing.

5 Divide the pasta salad among serving bowls and top with the hard-boiled eggs. Serve with the dressing.

300 g (10 oz) dried conchiglie pasta
200 g (7 oz) green beans, trimmed
4 hot-smoked peppered boneless mackerel fillets
125 g (4 oz) mixed salad
½ cucumber, cut in half lengthways, deseeded and cut into chunky pieces
2 spring onions, finely sliced
2 hard-boiled eggs, quartered

Dressing
100 ml (3½ fl oz) soured cream
1 tablespoon wholegrain mustard
1 teaspoon French mustard
2 tablespoons lemon juice
1 teaspoon chopped dill
1 teaspoon chopped tarragon
salt and pepper

Serves 4
Prep time **20 minutes, plus cooling**
Cooking time **10-12 minutes**

SEARED TUNA
WITH BEAN & ROCKET SALAD

1 Rub 1 tablespoon of the oil over the tuna steaks and season well with salt and pepper. Heat a griddle pan until smoking hot, then cook the tuna for 1–2 minutes on each side, or until charred on the outside but still pink in the middle. Alternatively, cook for a little less or longer until cooked to your liking.

2 Meanwhile, mix 2 tablespoons of the lemon juice with the remaining oil in a bowl and season to taste with salt and pepper. Toss with the remaining ingredients in a large bowl and add more lemon juice to taste.

3 Serve the bean salad with the seared tuna.

4 tablespoons olive oil
4 tuna steaks, about 150 g
  (5 oz) each
2–4 tablespoons lemon juice
finely grated rind of ½ lemon
2 x 400 g (13 oz) cans cannellini
  beans, drained
100 g (3½ oz) rocket leaves
1 small red onion, finely sliced
1 red chilli, deseeded and
  chopped
salt and pepper

Serves **4**
Prep time **10 minutes**
Cooking time **2–4 minutes**

Herbed Lamb
WITH FIG SALAD

2 tablespoons coriander seeds
2 tablespoons chopped
  rosemary
grated rind of 1 lemon
salt and black pepper
100 ml (3½ fl oz) olive oil
1 garlic clove, crushed
12 lamb cutlets
125 g (4 oz) rocket leaves
4 figs, sliced
75 g (3 oz) pitted black olives,
  halved
2-3 teaspoons lemon juice, to
  taste
yogurt, to serve

Serves 4
Prep time 15 minutes,
plus marinating
Cooking time 4-6 minutes

1 To make the rub, dry-fry the coriander seeds in a frying
  pan over a high heat for 2-3 minutes until they begin to
pop and release their aroma. Cool the coriander seeds and
mix with the rosemary, lemon rind and some salt and
pepper.

2 Put 2 tablespoons of the oil, the rub, the garlic and
  some salt and pepper in a large sealable plastic bag.
Add the lamb, toss well and seal the bag. Leave to marinate
in a cool box for 1-4 hours.

3 Remove the lamb from the marinade and pat dry.
  Transfer to a grill rack over a hot barbecue or campfire
and cook for about 2-3 minutes on each side, or until cooked
to your liking, then wrap loosely with foil and leave to rest
for 5 minutes.

4 Meanwhile, to make the salad, put the rocket, figs and
  olives in a large bowl and mix well. Whisk together the
remaining oil and 2-3 teaspoons lemon juice with some salt
and pepper. Add to the salad and stir to coat the leaves.
Serve with the lamb and some yogurt.

CYPRIOT CHICKEN
& Haloumi Salad

3 boneless, skinless chicken
  breast fillets, about 125 g
  (4 oz) each
1 bunch of oregano, chopped
1 tablespoon olive oil
250 g (8 oz) haloumi cheese
salt and pepper

Cypriot salad
1 cucumber, skinned, deseeded
  and cut lengthways into short
  batons
4 large tomatoes, skinned,
  deseeded and cut into wedges
1 red onion, finely chopped
1 bunch of flat leaf parsley,
  roughly chopped
3 tablespoons olive oil
1 tablespoon wine vinegar

Serves **4**
Prep time **20 minutes, plus**
marinating
Cooking time **about 25**
minutes

1 Put the chicken in a bowl, add the chopped oregano, olive oil and salt and pepper and toss together. Cover with clingfilm and leave to marinate in a cool box for 2 hours.

2 Transfer the chicken to a grill rack over a hot barbecue or campfire and cook for about 6-8 minutes on each side, or until cooked through. Transfer to a plate, cut into chunks, cover with foil and keep warm.

3 Meanwhile, to make the salad, put the cucumber, tomato wedges, chopped red onion and parsley in a bowl. Add the olive oil and wine vinegar, toss well and season to taste with salt and pepper.

4 Slice the haloumi into 8, then transfer to the grill rack and cook for about 4 minutes on each side. Serve with the chicken and salad.

CHICKPEA & HERB SALAD

1 Put the bulgar wheat in a heatproof bowl and cover with boiling water. Leave to stand until the water is absorbed, then drain well, pressing out as much moisture as possible with the back of a spoon. Leave to cool.

2 Mix together the oil, lemon juice, parsley, mint and salt and pepper in a large bowl. Add the chickpeas, tomatoes, onion, cucumber and bulgar wheat. Mix well, then add the feta, stirring lightly to avoid breaking up the cheese.

100 g (3½ oz) bulgar wheat
4 tablespoons olive oil
1 tablespoon lemon juice
2 tablespoons chopped flat leaf parsley
1 tablespoon chopped mint
400 g (13 oz) can chickpeas, drained
125 g (4 oz) cherry tomatoes, halved
1 tablespoon chopped mild onion
100 g (3½ oz) cucumber, diced
150 g (5 oz) feta cheese, diced
salt and pepper

Serves **4**
Prep time **20 minutes, plus standing and cooling**

ORANGE
& AVOCADO SALAD

4 large juicy oranges
2 small ripe avocados, peeled
  and stoned
2 teaspoons cardamom pods
3 tablespoons olive oil
1 tablespoon clear honey
pinch of ground allspice
2 teaspoons lemon juice
salt and pepper
sprigs of watercress, to garnish

Serves 4
Prep time **15 minutes**

1 Using a sharp knife, remove the peel and pith from the oranges. Working over a bowl to catch the juice, cut between the membranes to remove the segments. Slice the avocados and toss gently with the orange segments. Pile into serving bowls.

2 Reserve a few whole cardamom pods for garnishing. Crush the remainder using a pestle and mortar to extract the seeds or place them in a small bowl and crush with the end of a rolling pin. Pick out and discard the pods.

3 Mix the seeds with the oil, honey, allspice and lemon juice in a bowl. Season to taste with salt and pepper and stir in the reserved orange juice.

4 Garnish the salads with sprigs of watercress and the reserved cardamom pods and serve with the dressing spooned over the top.

RIBBONED CARROT *Salad*

4 carrots
2 celery sticks
1 bunch of spring onions
4 tablespoons olive oil
2 tablespoons lime juice
2 teaspoons caster sugar
¼ teaspoon dried chilli flakes
2 tablespoons chopped mint
50 g (2 oz) salted peanuts
salt and pepper

Serves 4
Prep time **15 minutes, plus soaking**

1 Half fill a medium bowl with very cold water, adding a few ice cubes if possible.

2 Scrub the carrots and pare off as many long ribbons as you can from each. Place the ribbons in the water. Cut the celery into 5 cm (2 inch) lengths. Cut each length into very thin slices. Cut the spring onions into 5 cm (2 inch) lengths and shred lengthways. Add the celery and spring onions to the water and leave to soak for 15-20 minutes until the vegetables curl up.

3 Mix together the oil, lime juice, sugar, chilli flakes and mint in a small bowl and season to taste with salt and pepper.

4 Thoroughly drain the vegetables and toss in a bowl with the dressing, peanuts and salt and pepper. Serve the salad immediately.

GRIDDLED HALOUMI
with Warm Couscous Salad

1 Heat 3 tablespoons of the oil in a frying pan, add the onions and two-thirds of the chilli and cook over a medium heat, stirring, for about 5 minutes until softened. Add the chickpeas and tomatoes and cook over a high heat for 3 minutes, stirring occasionally, until the chickpeas are heated through and the tomatoes are softened but still retaining their shape.

2 Meanwhile, put the couscous in a heatproof bowl, add enough boiling water to cover by 1 cm (½ inch) and mix in the salt. Cover with clingfilm and leave to stand for 5 minutes, then fluff up with a fork.

3 Heat a griddle pan until hot. Mix the remaining olive oil and chilli with the herbs in a shallow bowl. Add the haloumi slices and toss to coat, then transfer to the griddle pan and cook for about 2-3 minutes, turning once, until browned in places.

4 Stir the couscous into the chickpea mixture and cook for 1 minute to heat through. Pile on to plates and top with the haloumi slices.

5 tablespoons olive oil
2 red onions, thinly sliced
1 red chilli, roughly chopped
400 g (13 oz) can chickpeas, drained
175 g (6 oz) cherry tomatoes, halved
200 g (7 oz) couscous
½ teaspoon salt
3 tablespoons chopped parsley
1 tablespoon thyme leaves
375 g (12 oz) haloumi cheese, thickly sliced

Serves **4**
Prep time **10 minutes**
Cooking time **10 minutes**

EGG, BASIL & CHEESE
SALAD WITH CHERRY TOMATOES

2 tablespoons olive oil
2 eggs, beaten
2 handfuls of basil, roughly
  chopped
200 g (7 oz) feta cheese,
  crumbled
250 g (8 oz) cherry plum
  tomatoes, halved
80 g (3 oz) watercress
1 tablespoon balsamic vinegar
pepper

Serves **4**
Prep time **10 minutes**
Cooking time **2 minutes**

1 Heat 1 tablespoon of the oil in a frying pan and swirl around. Beat the eggs in a large jug with the basil and plenty of pepper, then pour into the pan in a thin layer and cook for about 2 minutes, or until golden and set. Remove and cut into thick strips.

2 Meanwhile, toss the feta, cherry tomatoes and watercress in a bowl. Mix the remaining oil with the balsamic vinegar, pour over the salad and toss to coat.

3 Add the omelette strips, toss to mix and serve while still warm.

Spicy SWEET POTATO & FETA SALAD

1 Heat a griddle pan until hot. Toss together 2 tablespoons of the oil and the sweet potatoes in a bowl. Season well with salt and pepper, then cook in the hot griddle pan for about 3 minutes on each side, or until tender and lightly charred.

2 Meanwhile, mix together the remaining oil and vinegar in a bowl and season to taste with salt and pepper. Add the spinach and onion and toss together.

3 Transfer the sweet potatoes to plates, top with the spinach and onion, feta, chilli and olives and serve.

5 tablespoons olive oil
2 sweet potatoes, thinly sliced
1 tablespoon white wine vinegar
150 g (5 oz) baby spinach leaves
1 tablespoon finely chopped red onion
125 g (4 oz) feta cheese, crumbled
1 red chilli, sliced
50 g (2 oz) pitted black olives
salt and pepper

Serves 4
Prep time 10 minutes
Cooking time about 6 minutes

REAL GUACAMOLE
with raw vegetables

2 large firm, ripe avocados
½ small red onion, finely
  chopped
2 tablespoons lime juice
3 tablespoons finely chopped
  fresh coriander
¼ teaspoon garlic powder
¼ teaspoon celery salt
pinch of cayenne pepper
½ teaspoon paprika
3 tomatoes, deseeded and
  finely chopped
few dashes of Tabasco
  (optional)
salt and pepper

To serve
350 g (11½ oz) carrots, cut into
  batons
350 g (11½ oz) cauliflower
  florets
4 celery sticks, cut into batons
250 g (8 oz) radishes, trimmed
125 g (4 oz) baby sweetcorn

Serves 4
Prep time **15 minutes**

1 Peel the avocados and remove the stones, then mash the
  flesh in a small bowl with the back of a fork to break it up.

2 Add the red onion, lime juice, coriander, garlic powder,
  celery salt and spices. Mix until almost smooth, with some
small lumps, then season with salt and pepper. Stir in the
tomatoes and add the Tabasco, if using.

3 Arrange the raw vegetables on a large plate and serve with
  the guacamole.

WARM
COURGETTE &
Lime Salad

1 tablespoon olive oil
grated rind and juice of 1 lime
1 garlic clove, finely chopped
2 tablespoons roughly chopped
  fresh coriander, plus extra to
  garnish
2 courgettes, about 325 g (11 oz)
  in total, cut into thin diagonal
  slices
salt and pepper

....

Serves **4**
Prep time **10 minutes**
Cooking time **10 minutes**

....

1 Mix together the oil, lime rind and juice, garlic, chopped coriander and salt and pepper in a sealable plastic bag. Add the courgette slices and toss in the oil mixture. Seal and set aside until ready to cook.

2 Heat a griddle pan until hot. Arrange as many courgette slices as will fit in a single layer over the base of the pan and cook for about 2–3 minutes, or until browned on the underside. Turn the slices over and brown on the other side. Transfer the slices to a serving dish, cover with foil and keep warm. Repeat with the remaining courgettes.

3 Pour any remaining dressing over the courgettes, sprinkle with a little extra chopped coriander to garnish and serve immediately.

BEER FLATBREADS
WITH CHEESE & ONIONS

1 Put the flour, salt, yeast, 3 tablespoons of the oil and the mustard in a bowl and stir in the ale. Mix with a round-bladed knife to make a soft dough, adding a little more ale or water if the dough is dry. Tip out on to a lightly floured board and knead for about 10 minutes until the dough is smooth and elastic. (If you've no surface to work on, work the dough in the bowl as best as you can.) Return the dough to the bowl, cover with a tea towel or clingfilm and leave in a warm place (near the fire if already lit) until the dough has doubled in size.

2 Meanwhile, heat the remaining oil in a frying pan, add the onions and cook over a low heat for about 15 minutes, stirring frequently, until soft and deep golden. Leave to cool.

3 Divide the dough into 12 pieces and roll out each on a floured board to a round about 16 cm (6½ inches) in diameter. Sprinkle the centres of 6 of the rounds with cheese and spoon the onions on top. Brush the edges lightly with water and press another round of dough on top so the filling is sandwiched. Flatten out with a rolling pin until the dough is so thin that the filling shows through.

4 Heat a large dry frying pan or griddle pan, add 1 bread and cook until pale golden on the underside. Flip the bread over and cook on the other side until the dough is cooked through, about 5-7 minutes in total. Wrap in foil and keep warm. Repeat with the remaining breads.

300 g (10 oz) strong white bread flour, plus extra for dusting
1 teaspoon salt
1 teaspoon fast-action dried yeast
4 tablespoons olive oil
2 teaspoons Dijon mustard
150 ml (¼ pint) strong ale
2 medium onions, chopped
100 g (3½ oz) Cheddar or Gruyère cheese, grated

Serves 6
Prep time **30 minutes, plus proving**
Cooking time **45-55 minutes**

CORN FLATBREADS WITH SWEETCORN & GRUYÈRE

100 g (3½ oz) masa harina flour
100 g (3½ oz) self-raising flour,
  plus extra for dusting
1 teaspoon salt
2 tablespoons olive oil

Topping
150 g (5 oz) Gruyère cheese,
  grated
125 g (4 oz) canned sweetcorn,
  drained
4 tomatoes, thinly sliced
1 Little Gem lettuce, shredded
sweet chilli sauce
soured cream

Serves 4
Prep time **20 minutes**
Cooking time **25-40 minutes**

1 Put the flours, salt and olive oil in a bowl and stir in 150 ml (¼ pint) cold water to make a soft dough. Divide the dough into 4 even-sized pieces and roll out each as thinly as possible on a well-floured board to rounds about 20 cm (8 inches) in diameter.

2 Heat a dry frying pan for 5 minutes, add 1 flatbread and cook for about 2-4 minutes on each side until pale golden and cooked through. Slide out of the pan on to a sheet of foil and keep warm. Repeat with the remaining flatbreads.

3 To heat through and serve, sprinkle a thin layer of cheese and sweetcorn over a flatbread and add several slices of tomato. Return to the stove or fire, either in the pan or on a sheet of foil, and heat through until the cheese starts to melt.

4 Scatter with shredded lettuce, drizzle with chilli sauce and a little soured cream and fold or roll up to serve.

5 Repeat with the remaining flatbreads and toppings.

CAMPING TIP

When you're drinking in your tent, a shoe makes a good beaker or mug holder and avoids spillages and soggy sleeping bags.

BALSAMIC
Braised Leeks
& PEPPERS

2 tablespoons olive oil
2 leeks, trimmed and cut into
   1 cm (½ inch) pieces
1 orange pepper, cored,
   deseeded and cut into 1 cm
   (½ inch) chunks
1 red pepper, cored, deseeded
   and cut into 1 cm (½ inch)
   chunks
3 tablespoons balsamic
   vinegar
handful of flat leaf parsley,
   chopped
salt and pepper

1 Heat the oil in a saucepan, add the leeks and peppers and stir well. Cover with a lid and cook very gently for 10 minutes.

2 Add the balsamic vinegar and cook, uncovered, for a further 10 minutes. The vegetables should be brown from the vinegar and all the liquid should have evaporated. Season well with salt and pepper, then stir in the chopped parsley just before serving.

Serves **4**
Prep time **5 minutes**
Cooking time **20 minutes**

Mustard & Thyme
SWEET POTATOES

6 sweet potatoes, about 250 g
  (8 oz) each, scrubbed

Mustard and thyme butter
125 g (4 oz) butter, softened
1 tablespoon wholegrain
  mustard
1 teaspoon chopped thyme
pepper

Serves **6**
Prep time **5 minutes**
Cooking time **40 minutes**

1 Wrap each potato in a double layer of foil, then tuck between hot coals or logs, allowing some of the coals or logs to cover the potatoes. Cook for about 40 minutes, or until tender, rotating the parcels several times during cooking.

2 Meanwhile, to make the mustard and thyme butter, put the butter, mustard, thyme and some pepper in a bowl and mash with a fork until evenly mixed. Set aside.

3 Carefully remove the potatoes from the foil parcels. Cut in half and serve topped with the butter.

FIRE-BAKED NEW
POTATOES
with green dressing

1 Put the potatoes on a large square of heavy-duty foil. Drizzle with 1 tablespoon of the oil and season with salt and pepper. Bring the foil up around the potatoes and seal well, then tuck the parcel between hot coals or logs to cook. This will take 1-2 hours depending on the intensity of the fire. Rotate the parcel several times during cooking so the potatoes cook evenly.

2 Mix together the herbs, capers, remaining oil, lemon juice, honey and a little salt and pepper in a small bowl.

3 Carefully unwrap the foil and spoon the dressing over the potatoes to serve.

500 g (1 lb) new potatoes, scrubbed and rinsed
100 ml (3½ fl oz) olive oil
large handful each of parsley and chives, chopped
2 tablespoons chopped mint
2 tablespoons capers, drained and chopped
1 tablespoon lemon juice
2 teaspoons clear honey
salt and pepper

Serves **4**
Prep time **10 minutes**
Cooking time **1-2 hours**

BALSAMIC-ROASTED TOMATOES

1 Put the tomatoes, cut side up, on a large piece of heavy-duty foil and drizzle with the oil and vinegar. Tear half the basil over the top, add the pine nuts and season with salt and pepper.

2 Bring the foil up around the tomatoes and seal well, then tuck between hot coals or logs to cook for about 30-40 minutes, or until softened. Rotate the parcel several times during cooking.

3 Toast the bread, cut side down, on a rack over the barbecue or campfire, until charred.

4 Carefully unwrap the foil and spoon the tomatoes on to the toast. Sprinkle with the remaining basil leaves and serve immediately.

12 plum tomatoes, halved
2 tablespoons olive oil
2 teaspoons balsamic vinegar
1 small bunch of basil
2 tablespoons pine nuts
4 slices of ciabatta bread
salt and pepper

Serves **4**
Prep time **10 minutes**
Cooking time **30-40 minutes**

Roasted RED ONIONS

handful each of bay leaves and thyme
8 small red onions, peeled
2 tablespoons olive oil
3 tablespoons balsamic glaze
salt and pepper

Serves **4**
Prep time **10 minutes**
Cooking time **1-1½ hours**

1 Scatter the herbs on to a large piece of heavy-duty foil and put the onions on top. Drizzle with the oil and season lightly with salt and pepper.

2 Bring the foil up around the onions and seal well, then tuck between hot coals or logs to cook for about 40-50 minutes, or until softened.

3 Carefully unwrap the foil and drizzle the onions with the balsamic glaze. Re-seal the parcel and return to the fire until the onions are soft.

PANZANELLA

ORIGINATING FROM TUSCANY, ITALY, THIS IS A POPULAR SUMMER DISH, WITH THE TOASTED BREAD SOAKING UP THE JUICES FROM THE TOMATOES AND OLIVE OIL AND VINEGAR DRESSING. THE RIPER THE TOMATOES, THE MORE JUICE THERE WILL BE, AND THE MORE DELICIOUS THE DISH.

4 slices of ciabatta bread
4 ripe tomatoes, cored and
  chopped
½ cucumber, deseeded, peeled
  and cubed
1 red onion, chopped
handful of chopped flat leaf
  parsley
1 tablespoon chopped pitted
  black olives
50 ml (2 fl oz) olive oil
1-2 tablespoons wine vinegar
juice of ½ lemon
salt and pepper

Serves 4
Prep time **15 minutes, plus standing**
Cooking time **5 minutes**

1 Toast the bread lightly in a griddle pan or on a rack over a barbecue or campfire, then tear into pieces and put in a large bowl. Add the tomatoes, cucumber, onion, parsley and olives.

2 Mix together the oil, vinegar and lemon juice in a bowl and season with salt and pepper.

3 Pour the dressing over the salad and mix well. Cover and leave to stand for at least 1 hour to allow the flavours to mingle.

CRUSHED MINTED PEAS

A COMPULSORY ACCOMPANIMENT TO THE BEST FISH AND CHIPS, THIS IS THE HOMEMADE ANSWER TO THE PALE, SLOPPY PEA PURÉE THAT IS OFTEN SOLD TO PARTNER BOUGHT FISH AND CHIPS.

400 g (13 oz) fresh peas, shelled
several sprigs of mint
2 tablespoons butter
2 tablespoons crème fraîche
salt and pepper

Serves 4-6
Prep time 10 minutes
Cooking time 5 minutes

1 Cook the peas with the mint in a large saucepan of boiling water for about 5 minutes, or until very tender. Drain and return to the pan, discarding the mint.

2 Stir in the butter and crème fraîche and use a fork to crush the peas roughly. Season to taste with salt and pepper and reheat gently.

GARLIC BREAD

4 tablespoons butter, softened
1 garlic clove, crushed
2 tablespoons thyme leaves, roughly chopped (optional)
1 white or wholemeal baguette
salt and pepper

Serves 4
Prep time 10 minutes
Cooking time about 15 minutes

1 Beat the softened butter with the garlic and thyme, if using, in a bowl and season with a little salt and pepper. Cut the baguette into thick slices, almost all the way through but leaving the base attached. Spread the butter thickly over each slice.

2 Wrap the baguette in foil and cook on a grill rack over a barbecue or campfire for about 15 minutes, turning the parcel occasionally. Alternatively, cook in a griddle pan on a camping stove.

Devilled
MUSHROOMS

1 Finely chop the spring onions, reserving the green tops. Heat the butter and oil in a frying pan, add the white chopped spring onions and the mushrooms and fry, stirring, for about 3-4 minutes, or until golden.

2 Stir in the Worcestershire sauce, mustard and tomato paste. Add 4 tablespoons of water, the Tabasco, if using, and a little salt and pepper and cook for 2 minutes, stirring, until the sauce is beginning to thicken.

3 Meanwhile, toast the bread on both sides in a griddle pan or on a rack over a barbecue or campfire. Transfer to plates.

4 Stir the green spring onion tops through the mushrooms and cook for 1 minute, then spoon over the toast and serve.

6 spring onions
4 tablespoons butter
1 tablespoon sunflower oil
425 g (14 oz) white mushrooms, sliced
2 tablespoons Worcestershire sauce
2 teaspoons wholegrain mustard
2 teaspoons tomato paste
a few drops of Tabasco sauce (optional)
4 slices of crusty bread
salt and pepper

Serves 4
Prep time **5 minutes**
Cooking time **10 minutes**

TABBOULEH
WITH FRUIT & NUTS

150 g (5 oz) bulgar wheat
75 g (3 oz) unsalted, shelled
  pistachio nuts
1 small red onion, finely
  chopped
3 garlic cloves, crushed
2 handfuls of flat leaf parsley,
  chopped
large handful of mint, chopped
finely grated rind and juice of 1
  lemon or lime
150 g (5 oz) ready-to-eat
  prunes, sliced
4 tablespoons olive oil
salt and pepper

1 Put the bulgar wheat in a heatproof bowl and cover with plenty of boiling water. Leave to stand for 15 minutes.

2 Meanwhile, mix together the pistachios, onion, garlic, parsley, mint, lemon or lime rind and juice and prunes in a large bowl.

3 Drain the bulgar wheat well, pressing out as much moisture as possible with the back of a spoon. Add to the other ingredients with the oil and toss together. Season to taste with salt and pepper and serve.

Serves 4
Prep time **10 minutes, plus standing**

Green Couscous
WITH SPICED
FRUIT SAUCE

500 ml (17 fl oz) hot vegetable
   stock
250 g (8 oz) couscous
75 g (3 oz) unsalted, shelled
   pistachio nuts, roughly
   chopped
2 spring onions, chopped
small handful of parsley,
   chopped
425 g (14 oz) can flageolet
   beans, drained
salt and pepper

Spiced fruit sauce
½ teaspoon saffron threads
1 tablespoon cardamom pods
2 teaspoons coriander seeds
½ teaspoon chilli powder
4 tablespoons flaked almonds
75 g (3 oz) ready-to-eat dried
   apricots, finely chopped

Serves **4**
Prep time **20 minutes, plus
standing**
Cooking time **2 minutes**

1 To make the sauce, put the saffron in a small cup and pour over 1 tablespoon boiling water. Leave to stand for 3 minutes.

2 Crush the cardamom pods using a pestle and mortar, or place the pods in a small bowl and crush with the end of a rolling pin. Pick out and discard the pods, then lightly crush the seeds.

3 Add the coriander seeds, chilli powder and almonds to the bowl and crush again. Stir in the apricots. Pour in the saffron and soaking liquid and 200 ml (7 fl oz) of the hot stock, season with salt and pepper and mix well. Transfer to a saucepan and heat through.

4 Meanwhile, put the couscous in a heatproof bowl and add the remaining hot stock. Cover with clingfilm and leave to stand for 5 minutes until the stock is absorbed, then fluff up with a fork. Stir in the pistachios, spring onions, parsley and beans and season to taste with salt and pepper. Serve with the fruit sauce.

Thai-dressed
TOFU ROLLS

1 Remove 8 leaves from the lettuce. Fill a large heatproof bowl with boiling water. Add the separated leaves and leave for 10 seconds. Rinse in cold water and drain well.

2 Finely shred the remaining lettuce and toss in a bowl with the tofu and mangetout.

3 Mix together the oil, soy sauce, lime juice, sugar, chilli, garlic and pepper in a separate bowl and add to the tofu mixture. Toss together gently, using two spoons.

4 Spoon a little mixture on to the centre of each blanched lettuce leaf, then roll up and serve.

1 small iceberg lettuce
275 g (9 oz) tofu, diced
100 g (3½ oz) mangetout,
   shredded lengthways
2 tablespoons olive oil
2 tablespoons light soy sauce
2 tablespoons lime juice
1 tablespoon muscovado sugar
1 Thai chilli, deseeded and sliced
1 garlic clove, crushed
pepper

Serves **4**
Prep time **15 minutes**

TORTILLAS
with chilli & aubergine yogurt

1 Heat the oil in a frying pan, add the aubergine and fry for about 10 minutes until golden. Drain and leave to cool.

2 Mix together the herbs, chilli, yogurt and mayonnaise in a bowl and season to taste with salt and pepper.

3 Arrange the fried aubergine slices over the tortillas and spread with the Greek yogurt mixture, then top with the cucumber slices. Roll up each tortilla, sprinkle with paprika and serve.

4 tablespoons olive oil
1 aubergine, thinly sliced
small handful of mint, chopped
small handful of parsley, chopped
2 tablespoons chopped chives
1 green chilli, deseeded and thinly sliced
200 ml (7 fl oz) Greek yogurt
2 tablespoons mayonnaise
2 large tortillas
7 cm (3 inch) length of cucumber, thinly sliced
salt and pepper
paprika, to garnish

Serves **2**
Prep time **10 minutes, plus cooling**
Cooking time **10 minutes**

CAMPING TIP

It doesn't take much moisture to ruin a toilet roll – keep them in sealable plastic containers or ziplock bags so they stay dry. Alternatively, hang them up on the inside of the tent for easy access – and just take what you need.

BEAN & PEPPER *Burritos*

3 red peppers, cored, deseeded
and cut into small chunks
400 g (13 oz) can black beans,
drained
½ bunch of spring onions,
chopped
4 tablespoons chopped fresh
coriander
1 tablespoon hot pepper sauce
100 g (3½ oz) Cheddar cheese,
grated
4 large tortilla wraps
salt

Serves 4
Prep time 15 minutes
Cooking time 35-45 mins

1 Heat a frying pan, add the peppers and cook for about 15 minutes, or until softened and lightly browned.

2 Tip the peppers into a bowl and add the beans, spring onions, coriander and pepper sauce. Mix well. Stir in the cheese and a little salt.

3 Spoon the mixture on to the centres of the tortilla wraps. Spread the filling out into a strip that comes about 3.5 cm (1½ inches) from the edges. Fold these edges over, then roll up each tortilla, starting from an unfolded end, to enclose the filling.

4 Wrap each tortilla in heavy-duty foil, then tuck the parcels between hot coals or logs to cook for about 20-30 minutes until cooked through, turning the parcels occasionally so they cook evenly.

CAMPING TIP

Take a thin doormat to place by the tent door so you don't traipse too much water and mud inside. If you don't have a doormat — or you're short of space — you could use a mat from the car.

Sweet Potato, BACON & THYME CAKES

1 Cook the sweet potatoes in a saucepan of boiling water for about 5 minutes, or until soft. Drain well, then return to the pan and mash well. Tip into a bowl.

2 Meanwhile, heat 1 tablespoon of the oil in a frying pan, add the diced bacon and fry until crisp. Using a slotted spoon, add to the sweet potatoes, reserving the oil in the pan.

3 Add the thyme, egg and buttermilk to the sweet potato mixture and beat together to make a smooth batter. Add the flour and stir until evenly mixed.

4 Reheat the frying pan until hot. Scoop large spoonfuls of the mixture into the pan, spacing them slightly apart, and cook until golden on the underside, then turn the cakes over and cook on the other side until golden and cooked through. Remove from the pan and serve warm, drizzled with maple syrup or chilli sauce.

5 Repeat with the remaining mixture, adding a little more oil to the pan as required.

250 g (8 oz) sweet potatoes, cut into small chunks
1-2 tablespoons vegetable oil
125 g (4 oz) streaky bacon, finely diced
1 tablespoon chopped thyme
1 egg
150 ml (¼ pint) buttermilk
175 g (6 oz) self-raising flour
maple syrup or sweet chilli sauce, to serve

Serves **4**
Prep time **15 minutes**
Cooking time **about 20-30 minutes**

5 WAYS WITH...

Make the most of some classic and versatile camping ingredients with these quick, easy and delicious meals and snacks that mean you'll never be without a bite to eat.

EGGS

1. You can't beat a bacon and egg butty for a classic camping breakfast. Cook the bacon and eggs together in one large frying pan and serve between doorstop bread slices.

2. Soft-boiled egg dippers can be served with toast soldiers or breadsticks, or try with steamed asparagus for a grown-up treat.

3. Scrambled eggs served in croissants, muffins or wraps make a fuss-free meal.

4. Frittatas are easy to cook when camping and they're a great way of using up any leftover vegetables on the last day.

5. Huevos rancheros (ranch eggs) is the perfect camping recipe: fried onion, chilli, garlic, peppers and courgettes are fried with a can of tomatoes. Make a couple of wells in the mix, crack in 2 eggs and simmer until the eggs are cooked through. Sprinkle with coriander to serve.

BAKED BEANS

1 Cook away the liquid until the sauce is thick and the beans are stodgy. Add some grated cheese and roll up the mixture in a wrap.

2 Cook a one-pot bean casserole with sausages, a dash of Worcestershire sauce and a good dollop of mustard.

3 Add chilli and any other spices to your beans and serve with baked potatoes or crusty bread.

4 Mash baked beans with boiled (and drained) potatoes and make patties to cook in a griddle pan or frying pan over the campfire.

5 For a quick, filling and hassle-free meal, heat a can of beans, cook some pasta and combine the two ingredients.

CANNED TOMATOES

1 Reduce down a can of tomatoes – with a dash of balsamic, some garlic and basil, if you have them – and use as a 'pizza' topping on pitta bread, halved baguettes or wraps.

2 Add a dash of Worcestershire sauce and serve the tomatoes on toast.

3 Make a ratatouille with fried onion, peppers and a can of tomatoes and serve with baked potatoes, meat or rice. It also tastes great served cold, so it's perfect for a lunch of leftovers.

4 Add a can of drained kidney beans (and courgette or red pepper if you have them) and a pinch of dried chilli or chilli flakes to a can of tomatoes and simmer for 10 minutes for a quick and easy veggie chilli.

5 Make a hearty soup or stew with canned tomatoes and any meat or vegetables you have in the camping pantry. You could also add a handful of cooked rice or pasta for a more substantial meal.

FRESH TOMATO SAUCE

1 Put the tomatoes in a heatproof bowl, cover with boiling water and leave for about 2 minutes, or until the skins start to split. Pour away the water. Peel and roughly chop the tomatoes.

2 Heat the oil in a large saucepan, add the onion and cook over a medium heat for about 5 minutes until softened but not browned. Add the garlic and fry for a further 1 minute.

3 Add the tomatoes and cook for 20-25 minutes, stirring frequently, until the sauce is thickened and pulpy.

4 Stir in the oregano and season to taste with salt and pepper. If the sauce is very sharp, add a sprinkling of caster sugar.

1 kg (2 lb) very ripe, full-flavoured tomatoes
100 ml (3½ fl oz) olive oil
1 onion, finely chopped
2 garlic cloves, crushed
2 tablespoons chopped oregano
sprinkling of caster sugar (optional)
salt and pepper

Serves 4
Prep time **15 minutes**
Cooking time **30 minutes**

Chasseur SAUCE

3 tablespoons butter
200 g (7 oz) button mushrooms, thinly sliced
2 shallots, finely chopped
2 teaspoons plain flour
150 ml (¼ pint) dry white wine
300 ml (½ pint) beef or chicken stock
2 tablespoons finely chopped chervil or tarragon
1 tablespoon brandy (optional)
salt and pepper

Serves 4
Prep time **10 minutes**
Cooking time **25 minutes**

1 Melt the butter in a large saucepan until foaming, add the mushrooms and shallots and cook for 5 minutes until lightly browned. Transfer the mushrooms to a plate with a slotted spoon, leaving any small pieces of shallot in the pan.

2 Add the flour to the pan and cook for 2 minutes, stirring constantly, until it begins to darken in colour. Remove from the heat and gradually blend in the wine, then the stock.

3 Return to the heat and bring to the boil, then simmer gently for 15 minutes until the sauce is slightly thickened. Stir in the mushrooms, chervil or tarragon, brandy, if using, and salt and pepper to taste. Serve hot.

AMATRICIANA
Sauce

THIS IS A GOOD CHOICE FOR THOSE WHO LIKE THEIR TOMATO SAUCE TO HAVE A PUNCHIER FLAVOUR. IF THE TOMATOES ARE LACKING IN FLAVOUR, STIR IN A GENEROUS DOLLOP OF SUN-DRIED TOMATO PASTE.

1 kg (2 lb) ripe, full-flavoured tomatoes
5 tablespoons olive oil
1 large onion, finely chopped
1 celery stick, finely chopped
75 g (3 oz) pancetta, cubed
3 garlic cloves, crushed
1 hot red chilli, deseeded and finely chopped
salt and pepper

Serves 4
Prep time **10 minutes**
Cooking time **40 minutes**

1 Put the tomatoes in a heatproof bowl, cover with boiling water and leave for about 2 minutes, or until the skins start to split. Pour away the water. Peel and roughly chop the tomatoes.

2 Heat the oil in a large saucepan, add the onion, celery and pancetta and fry gently for 6–8 minutes, stirring frequently, until softened. Add the garlic and chilli and fry for a further 2 minutes.

3 Stir in the chopped tomatoes and cook gently, uncovered, for about 30 minutes, stirring frequently, or until the sauce is very thick and pulpy. Season with salt and pepper to taste and serve.

PUTTANESCA SAUCE

THIS INTENSE ITALIAN TOMATO SAUCE HAS PLENTY OF EXTRA FLAVOURS SUCH AS BLACK OLIVES, ANCHOVIES AND CHILLIES. THICK AND RICH, IT'S GREAT TOSSED WITH ALMOST ANY PASTA, ESPECIALLY SPAGHETTI.

1 Heat the oil in a large saucepan, add the onion and cook over a medium heat for about 5 minutes until softened. Add the garlic and chilli and cook for a further 1 minute.

2 Add the anchovy fillets, tomatoes, sugar and black olives and bring to the boil, then simmer gently for 10 minutes until the sauce is thick.

3 Add the basil leaves, capers and a little salt and heat through, stirring, for 1 minute. Serve hot, sprinkled with Parmesan cheese, if liked.

4 tablespoons olive oil
1 onion, finely chopped
3 garlic cloves, crushed
1 small red chilli, deseeded and finely chopped
6 anchovy fillets, chopped
2 x 400 g (13 oz) cans chopped tomatoes
½ teaspoon caster sugar
75 g (3 oz) black olives, pitted and finely chopped
small handful of basil leaves
2 tablespoons capers, drained
salt
grated Parmesan cheese, to serve (optional)

Serves **4**
Prep time **15 minutes**
Cooking time **15 minutes**

Tomato & Mushroom SAUCE

1 Put the tomatoes in a heatproof bowl, cover with boiling water and leave for about 2 minutes, or until the skins start to split. Pour away the water. Peel and roughly chop the tomatoes.

2 Heat the oil in a large saucepan, add the onion and garlic and cook over a low heat, stirring frequently, until the onion is soft. Add the tomatoes, oregano and a little salt and pepper.

3 Bring to a simmer, then cover with a lid and cook gently for about 10 minutes. Add the mushrooms and cook for a further 5 minutes until thickened and pulpy. Break up the tomatoes frequently during cooking.

4 Adjust the seasoning if necessary and serve immediately.

1 kg (2 lb) ripe tomatoes
75 ml (3 fl oz) olive oil
1 large onion, finely chopped
1 garlic clove, finely chopped
2 tablespoons chopped oregano
200 g (7 oz) chestnut
   mushrooms, finely sliced
salt and pepper

Serves 4-6
Prep time **15 minutes**
Cooking time **25 minutes**

BOLOGNESE SAUCE

2 tablespooons butter
2 tablespoons olive oil
1 onion, finely chopped
2 celery sticks, finely chopped
2 garlic cloves, crushed
500 g (1 lb) lean minced beef
200 g (7 oz) spicy Italian
  sausages, skins removed
300 ml (½ pint) red or white
  wine
400 g (13 oz) can chopped
  tomatoes
1 teaspoon caster sugar
2 bay leaves
1 teaspoon dried oregano
2 tablespoons sun-dried
  tomato paste
salt and pepper

Serves **4–6**
Prep time **15 minutes**
Cooking time **1¼ hours**

COMBINING ITALIAN-STYLE SPICY SAUSAGES WITH THE MORE FAMILIAR MINCED BEEF GIVES THIS SAUCE A RICH MEATY FLAVOUR REMINISCENT OF THE TRADITIONAL SAUCE SERVED IN BOLOGNA. ALLOW TIME FOR LONG, GENTLE COOKING TO TENDERIZE THE MEAT AND LET THE FLAVOURS MINGLE.

1 Heat the butter and oil in a large saucepan, add the onion and celery and cook over a medium heat for about 5 minutes until softened. Add the garlic, beef and skinned sausages and cook until they are lightly coloured, breaking up the beef and the sausages with a wooden spoon.

2 Add the wine and let it bubble for 1–2 minutes until slightly evaporated. Add the tomatoes, sugar, bay leaves, oregano, tomato paste and a little salt and pepper and bring just to the boil. Cover with a lid and cook over a very low heat for about 1 hour, stirring occasionally, until thick, pulpy and cooked through.

CHORIZO CHERRY TOMATO SAUCE

ADDING PIECES OF SPICY CHORIZO SAUSAGE TO A TOMATO SAUCE IS ONE OF THE EASIEST AND TASTIEST WAYS OF GIVING IT PLENTY OF BOLD FLAVOUR. THIS SAUCE IS DELICIOUS WITH ALMOST ANY WHITE FISH.

1 Heat the oil in a saucepan, add the onion and fry gently, stirring, for about 3 minutes until beginning to soften. Add the chorizo and fennel or celery seeds and fry for a further 2 minutes.

2 Strain the cherry tomatoes through a sieve into the pan, reserving the whole pieces. Add the vinegar, honey and a little salt and pepper to the pan and bring to the boil. Cover with a lid and cook over a low heat for 8 minutes.

3 Add the strained tomatoes and adjust the seasoning if necessary. Heat through for 1 minute and serve hot.

3 tablespoons olive oil
1 large red onion, finely chopped
125 g (4 oz) chorizo sausage, finely diced
1 teaspoon fennel or celery seeds
400 g (13 oz) can cherry tomatoes
1 tablespoon wine vinegar
1 tablespoon clear honey
salt and pepper

Serves **4**
Prep time **10 minutes**
Cooking time **15 minutes**

SAUCE VIERGE

MIX THE SAUCE A COUPLE OF HOURS IN ADVANCE SO IT'S READY TO HEAT THROUGH GENTLY BEFORE SERVING.

1 Put the tomatoes in a heatproof bowl, cover with boiling water and leave for about 2 minutes, or until the skins start to split. Pour away the water. Peel the tomatoes, then halve them and scoop out the seeds with a teaspoon. Chop the flesh into small dice.

2 Using a pestle and mortar or the end of a rolling pin, crush the coriander seeds as finely as possible. Discard the stalks from the herbs and finely chop the leaves.

3 Mix together the diced tomatoes, coriander seeds, herbs, garlic, lemon rind and juice, and oil with a little salt and pepper in a bowl. Cover with clingfilm and store in a cool box. Heat through over a medium heat when ready to serve.

4 ripe tomatoes
½ teaspoon coriander seeds
large handful of fresh herbs (such as chervil, flat leaf parsley, tarragon and chives)
1 garlic clove, finely chopped
finely grated rind and juice of 1 lemon
100 ml (3½ fl oz) olive oil
salt and pepper

Serves **6**
Prep time **5 minutes**
Cooking time **2 minutes**

LEMON & VODKA SAUCE

THIS SPICY SAUCE, ENLIVENED WITH CHILLI AND VODKA, IS REALLY GOOD
SERVED WITH FRESH LINGUINE OR VERMICELLI, TOPPED WITH TOASTED FLAKED
ALMONDS AND EXTRA THYME, IF LIKED.

1 Pare thin strips of rind from the lemon using a lemon zester or sharp knife. Squeeze 1 tablespoon lemon juice.

2 Heat the oil in a saucepan, add the lemon rind, garlic, chilli and thyme and fry gently for 2-3 minutes, or until the ingredients start to colour.

3 Add the cream cheese to the saucepan and heat through until it softens to the consistency of pouring cream. Stir in the vodka, lemon juice and a little salt and serve hot.

1 lemon
2 tablespoons olive oil
2 garlic cloves, thinly sliced
1 red chilli, deseeded and thinly sliced
2 teaspoons chopped thyme, plus a little extra to garnish
100 g (3½ oz) cream cheese
2 tablespoons vodka
salt

Serves **2**
Prep time **10 minutes**
Cooking time **5 minutes**

DILL & MUSTARD
SAUCE

THIS SWEDISH SAUCE IS SWEET BUT TANGY AND STRONGLY FLAVOURED WITH DILL. IT CAN BE MADE AHEAD AND KEEPS WELL IN A COOL BOX FOR A COUPLE OF DAYS. SERVE IT WITH HOT OR COLD SMOKED FISH, PARTICULARLY SALMON, OR WITH A WARM, NEW POTATO SALAD. LEFTOVERS ARE DELICIOUS WITH SALADS OR IN COLD MEAT SANDWICHES.

1 Pull the dill from the sprigs and chop finely. Put the mustards, sugar and vinegar into a bowl and add a little salt.

2 Whisking constantly, gradually add the oil in a steady stream until the sauce is thick and smooth.

3 Stir in the dill, then taste and adjust the seasoning, adding a little more salt, vinegar or sugar, if liked.

large handful of dill
2 tablespoons mild, wholegrain mustard
1 teaspoon Dijon mustard
2 tablespoons caster sugar
3 tablespoons white wine vinegar
150 ml (¼ pint) olive oil
salt

Serves **8**
Prep time **10 minutes**

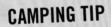

CAMPING TIP

Put a picnic or travel rug underneath your air bed or camping mat. This stops all the heat disappearing directly into the ground and makes for a much cosier night under the stars.

**SWEET & SOUR SPICED
PINEAPPLE & MANGO**

**CHOCOLATE &
BANANA MELTS**

MULLED CRANBERRY & RED WINE

QUICK KIWIFRUIT CHEESECAKES

SWEET STUFF & DRINKS

HOT BARBECUED
Fruit Salad

1 Top and tail the pineapple and place it on one end on a chopping board. Using a sharp knife, cut downwards to remove the skin, working all around the pineapple. Cut the pineapple flesh into chunks – in a small pineapple the core is usually sweet and soft enough to eat.

2 Peel the mango and cut it into slices on either side of the stone. Cook the mango and pineapple on a grill rack over a hot barbecue or campfire for 4 minutes on each side and the nectarine, peach and apricots for 3 minutes on each side, until lightly charred. If you like, thread the fruit pieces on to metal skewers before cooking.

3 Serve the griddled fruit topped with Greek yogurt, drizzled with clear honey and scattered with cardamom seeds, if using.

1 small pineapple
1 mango
1 nectarine, quartered and pitted
1 peach, quartered and pitted
2 apricots, halved, or quartered if large, and pitted
4 tablespoons Greek yogurt
clear honey, for drizzling
few cardamom seeds (optional)

Serves 4
Prep time 15 minutes
Cooking time 8 minutes

Fruit Salad KEBABS

1 Put all the syrup ingredients and 125 ml (4 fl oz) water in a small saucepan and bring slowly to the boil, stirring occasionally, until the sugar has dissolved, then boil rapidly for 1 minute. Leave to cool slightly.

2 Cut the green top off the pineapple, then cut away the skin. Cut into 8 wedges, cutting through the top down to the base. Remove the core, then thickly slice the wedges. Put the fruit into a shallow dish.

3 Quarter the papaya and scoop out the black seeds with a spoon. Peel away the skin, then thickly slice. Cut the peach into chunks and halve the strawberries. Mix all the fruit together in a bowl and pour the warm syrup over. Cover with clingfilm and leave to infuse for 1 hour, or overnight, if preferred.

4 Thread the fruit on to 8 metal skewers (or wooden skewers that have been soaked in cold water for 30 minutes) and cook on a grill rack over a hot barbecue or campfire for about 10 minutes, turning several times and brushing with the syrup, until hot and browned around the edges.

5 Serve the kebabs with spoonfuls of yogurt mixed with a little of the syrup, if liked.

½ large pineapple
1 papaya
1 peach, halved and pitted
8 large strawberries, hulled
Greek yogurt, to serve

Syrup
¼ teaspoon Chinese 5-spice powder
100 g (3½ oz) light brown sugar
grated rind and juice of 1 lemon

Serves 4
Prep time **20 minutes, plus marinating**
Cooking time **15 minutes**

GRIDDLED PEACHES
WITH PASSION FRUIT

1 Cook the peach halves, cut side down, on a grill rack over a hot barbecue or campfire for about 3-4 minutes, or until lightly charred. Turn the peaches over, drizzle with the honey and dust with cinnamon, then cook for a further 2 minutes, or until softened.

2 Transfer to bowls and serve topped with Greek yogurt and the passion fruit pulp.

6 large ripe peaches, halved and pitted
2 tablespoons clear honey, plus extra to serve
2 teaspoons ground cinnamon

To serve
125 g (4 oz) Greek yogurt
pulp from 2 passion fruit

Serves **4**
Prep time **5 minutes**
Cooking time **about 5 minutes**

Creole
PINEAPPLE WEDGES

1 small pineapple, about 1.25 kg
   (2½ lb)
1 tablespoon dark rum
juice of 1 lime
15 g (½ oz) sesame seeds

Serves **4**
Prep time **10 minutes**
Cooking time **10 minutes**

1 Cut the pineapple lengthways, first in half and then into quarters, leaving the leaves intact. The wedges should be about 1 cm (½ inch) thick, so it may be necessary to divide the quarters again.

2 Mix together the dark rum and lime juice in a bowl, then sprinkle the mixture over the pineapple slices.

3 Cook the pineapple on a grill rack over a hot barbecue or campfire for about 10 minutes, turning to ensure even cooking. Serve sprinkled with sesame seeds.

CAMPING TIP

Solar-powered fairy lights not only make your tent look pretty but also act as a handy guide home when you're wandering back in the middle of the night, especially if you're on a busy site with a hundred identical tents.

MINI STRAWBERRY
Shortcakes

250 g (8 oz) cream cheese
2 teaspoons icing sugar
8 digestive biscuits or
  homemade biscuits (see
  page 11)
4 teaspoons strawberry jam
250 g (8 oz) strawberries,
  hulled and sliced

Serves 4
Prep time **20 minutes, plus
chilling**

1 Beat the cream cheese in a bowl to soften, then stir in the icing sugar.

2 Spread a biscuit with 1 teaspoon of the strawberry jam, then spread a quarter of the cream cheese mixture over the biscuit. Lay a few strawberry slices on top of the cream cheese, then top with a second biscuit. Repeat to make 3 more shortcakes.

3 Transfer to a plastic box with a lid and chill in a cool box for a least 1 hour before serving.

Tipsy Blueberry Pots & MASCARPONE

1 Mix together three-quarters of the blueberries and the alcohol in a bowl, cover with clingfilm and leave to soak for at least 1 hour. Mash the blueberries.

2 Beat together the mascarpone and yogurt in a separate bowl until smooth, then mix in the sugar and lime rind and juice.

3 Layer alternate spoonfuls of mashed blueberries and mascarpone in bowls or glasses, top with the whole blueberries and serve.

200 g (7 oz) blueberries
2 tablespoons kirsch or vodka
150 g (5 oz) mascarpone cheese
150 g (5 oz) natural yogurt
2 tablespoons caster sugar
grated rind and juice of 1 lime

Serves **4**
Prep time **15 minutes, plus soaking**

CAMPING TIP

Campers always underestimate how many coins they need for the showers and 20 pence pieces will become like gold dust if your campsite charges for showers, tumble dryers or anything else for that matter!

SWEET & SOUR SPICED
Pineapple & Mango

1 firm, ripe mango
1 small pineapple, sliced in half
  lengthways and then into thin
  wedges
2 tablespoons icing sugar, plus
  extra to serve

Sweet and sour dressing
½ long red chilli, deseeded and
  finely chopped
4 tablespoons lime juice
2 tablespoons soft light brown
  sugar
1-2 tablespoons finely shredded
  mint

Serves 4
Prep time **10 minutes**
Cooking time **8 minutes**

1 Heat a griddle pan over a medium-high heat.

2 Cut the mango into 2 pieces, using the stone as a guide and cutting either side of it. Sift icing sugar all over the cut sides of the mango and pineapple so they are well covered.

3 Lay the mango, cut side down, and pineapple in the hot pan and griddle for 2 minutes, twisting the pieces once so that a charred criss-cross pattern appears on the fruit. Turn the pineapple wedges over and repeat on the other side. This may need to be done in two batches.

4 Meanwhile, to make the sweet and sour dressing, put the chilli, lime juice, sugar and mint in a small bowl, then stir until the sugar is dissolved. Set aside.

5 Transfer the fruits to plates and drizzle over the dressing. Serve dusted with extra icing sugar, if liked.

PASSION FRUIT YOGURT FOOL

200 ml (7 fl oz) whipping cream
6 passion fruit, halved, flesh
   and seeds removed
300 ml (½ pint) Greek yogurt
1 tablespoon clear honey
4 pieces of shortbread or
   homemade biscuits (see
   page 11), to serve

Serves 4
Prep time 8 minutes

1 Whip the cream in a bowl until it forms soft peaks.

2 Put the passion fruit flesh and seeds, yogurt and honey in a separate bowl and stir together, then fold in the cream.

3 Spoon into tall glasses or bowls and serve with the biscuits.

FIGS
WITH YOGURT
& HONEY

8 ripe figs
4 tablespoons natural yogurt
2 tablespoons clear honey

Serves 4
Prep time 5 minutes
Cooking time 10 minutes

1 Heat a griddle pan until hot. Slice the figs in half, then add to the pan, skin side down, and cook for 10 minutes until the skins begin to blacken.

2 Serve the figs with spoonfuls of yogurt and some honey spooned over the top.

LEMON & PASSION FRUIT WHIPS

50 g (2 oz) shortbread biscuits,
  crushed
150 ml (¼ pint) double cream
120 g (4 oz) pot lemon yogurt
2 passion fruit, halved

Serves **2**
Prep time **10 minutes**

1 Divide the crushed biscuits between two glasses or bowls.
Whip the cream in a bowl until just thick enough to form soft
peaks, then lightly fold in the yogurt with the seeds and pulp
from 1 of the passion fruit.

2 Spoon the mixture into the glasses, spoon the remaining
passion fruit seeds and pulp over the top and serve.

STEWED RHUBARB
with Custard

1 Put the rhubarb, orange juice or water and ground ginger, if using, in a large saucepan. Add as much of the remaining sugar as you like, depending on sweetness desired, to the rhubarb. Heat until the sugar has dissolved, then simmer gently, stirring occasionally, for about 8 minutes, or until the rhubarb is tender. Remove from the heat and leave to cool slightly.

2 Heat the custard in a separate saucepan according to the packet instructions.

3 Spoon the rhubarb into bowls and serve with the custard.

750 g (1½ lb) rhubarb, cut into 3.5 cm (1½ inch) lengths
3 tablespoons orange juice or water
½ teaspoon ground ginger (optional)
50–100 g (2–3½ oz) caster sugar
600 ml (1 pint) ready-made custard

Serves 4–6
Prep time 5 minutes
Cooking time 15 minutes

BLUEBERRY & ORANGE
Eton Mess

1 Put the custard, yogurt, orange rind and vanilla bean paste or extract in a bowl and stir until well combined.

2 Put two-thirds of the blueberries in four glasses or bowls. Spoon over the blueberry yogurt mixture, then top each glass with a lightly crushed meringue. Sprinkle over the remaining blueberries and serve immediately.

250 ml (8 fl oz) fresh vanilla custard
200 g (7 oz) blueberry yogurt
1 teaspoon finely grated orange rind
1 teaspoon vanilla bean paste or extract
150 g (5 oz) blueberries
4 ready-made meringues nests

Serves 4
Prep time 10 minutes

CINNAMON & RAISIN PEAR TRIFLE

1 Put the raisins, half of the cinnamon and 100 ml (3½ fl oz) of the juice from the pears in a saucepan over a medium-high heat and bring up to a gentle boil, then simmer over a low heat for 1 minute. Turn off the heat and leave to stand for 5 minutes.

2 Beat the custard with the remaining cinnamon in a bowl and slice the pears into thick pieces.

3 Place the panettone in the bottom of four bowls. Pour the warm raisin mixture over the panettone cubes and cover with the sliced pears. Pour over the custard, cover with clingfilm and chill in a cool box for about 10 minutes.

4 Spoon 1 tablespoon of the crème fraîche over each trifle and serve scattered with the hazelnuts.

75 g (3 oz) raisins
1 teaspoon cinnamon
400 g (13 oz) can pears in juice
500 g (1 lb) fresh vanilla custard
175 g (6 oz) panettone, cut into
  bite-sized cubes
4 tablespoons crème fraîche
50 g (2 oz) roasted hazelnuts,
  roughly chopped

Serves 4
Prep time **20 minutes**,
plus chilling
Cooking time **5 minutes**

CHOCOLATE & BANANA MELTS

1 Place half the bread slices on a board and top each with the chocolate, banana and marshmallows. Top with the remaining bread.

2 Brush the sandwiches lightly with oil and cook on a grill rack over a barbecue or campfire for 1-2 minutes. Flip the sandwiches over and cook for a further 1-2 minutes until golden.

8 slices of white bread, crusts removed
75 g (3 oz) dark chocolate, finely chopped
1 large banana, sliced
50 g (2 oz) marshmallows, chopped
vegetable oil, for brushing

Serves **4**
Prep time **5 minutes**
Cooking time **2-4 minutes**

COOKING TIP

If you're feeling really lazy, just make a slit in each banana skin, pop a couple of squares of chocolate in, and grill away until softened.

BLUEBERRY & GINGER
PATTIES

1 Put the flour and baking powder in a bowl, add the butter and rub in with the fingertips until the mixture resembles fine breadcrumbs. Stir in the ginger, blueberries and sugar.

2 Add the milk to the bowl and mix with a round-bladed knife to make a soft dough. Turn out on to a lightly floured board and shape into a log. Cut across into 12 pieces, all roughly the same size and about 1 cm (½ inch) thick.

3 Heat a little oil in a frying pan, add several of the patties and cook until golden on the underside. Turn the patties over and cook for a further few minutes until golden and cooked through. Remove from the pan, lightly dust with sugar and serve warm with clotted cream or yogurt.

4 Repeat with the remaining patties, adding a little more oil to the pan as required.

200 g (7 oz) self-raising flour, plus extra for dusting
1 teaspoon baking powder
50 g (2 oz) slightly salted butter, cubed
2 pieces of stem ginger, finely chopped
75 g (3 oz) dried blueberries
25 g (1 oz) caster sugar, plus extra for dusting
75 ml (3 fl oz) milk
vegetable oil, for frying
clotted cream or Greek yogurt, to serve

Serves **4**
Prep time **20 minutes**
Cooking time **15-20 minutes**

S'mores

200 g (7 oz) milk chocolate, broken into pieces
18 marshmallows
plenty of bought or homemade sweet biscuits (see page 11)

Makes **about 18**
Prep time **20 minutes**
Cooking time **3 minutes**

1 Put the chocolate in a heatproof bowl and place on a grill rack over the coolest area of a barbecue or campfire.

2 Thread the marshmallows on to several metal skewers, leaving a space between each, then heat over the fire, turning them until lightly toasted.

3 For each 's'more', spread a little melted chocolate on to a biscuit, top with a toasted marshmallow and then another chocolate-coated biscuit, pressing the biscuits together gently so the marshmallow spreads to form a filling.

CHOC CINNAMON
Eggy Bread

2 eggs
2 thick slices of seeded brown
  bread, cut in half
1 tablespoon butter
2 tablespoons caster sugar
2 teaspoons cocoa powder
½ teaspoon ground cinnamon

Serves **2**
Prep time **2 minutes**
Cooking time **5 minutes**

1 Lightly beat the eggs in a shallow dish. Dip the bread slices in the mixture, turning them over so they've absorbed the batter on both sides.

2 Melt the butter in a frying pan until foaming, add the eggy bread and cook for about 5 minutes, turning occasionally, until golden on both sides.

3 Mix the sugar, cocoa powder and cinnamon on a plate. Transfer the hot eggy bread to the plate and coat in the mixture. Serve immediately.

COOKING TIP

Serve with the glossy chocolate sauce on page 246 for a chocoholic's dream dish!

QUICK KIWIFRUIT
& Ginger Cheesecakes

75 g (3 oz) gingernut biscuits
100 g (3½ oz) cream cheese
75 g (3 oz) crème fraîche
1 piece of stem ginger, about
 15 g (½ oz), chopped
1 tablespoon stem ginger syrup
2 kiwifruit, peeled and sliced

1 Put the gingernut biscuits in a plastic bag and crush them using a rolling pin. Sprinkle the crushed biscuits over the bottom of four glasses or bowls.

2 Beat the cream cheese, crème fraîche, stem ginger and syrup in a bowl, then spoon the mixture over the biscuits. Arrange the kiwifruit on top of the cheesecakes and serve.

Serves **4**
Prep time **10 minutes**

Glossy
CHOCOLATE SAUCE

1 Put the sugar and 125 ml (4 fl oz) water in a small saucepan and cook over a low heat, stirring constantly with a wooden spoon, until the sugar has completely dissolved.

2 Bring the syrup to the boil and boil for 1 minute, then remove the pan from the heat and leave to cool for 1 minute. Tip the chocolate into the pan.

3 Add the butter and leave until the chocolate and butter have melted, stirring frequently, until the sauce is smooth and glossy. If the last of the chocolate doesn't melt completely or you want to serve the sauce warm, return the pan briefly to a very low heat.

125 g (4 oz) caster sugar
200 g (7 oz) plain dark
  chocolate, chopped
2 tablespoons unsalted butter

Serves **4-6**
Prep time **5 minutes**
Cooking time **about 5 minutes**

Apple Sauce

4 tablespoons butter
3 large cooking apples, peeled, cored and chopped
50 g (2 oz) caster sugar
6 whole cloves
finely grated rind and juice of 1 lemon
salt

Serves **6**
Prep time **10 minutes**
Cooking time **20 minutes**

1 Melt the butter in a saucepan and add the apples, sugar, cloves, lemon rind and juice and a little salt. Cover with a lid and leave to cook gently over the lowest heat for about 20 minutes, stirring the mixture occasionally, until the apples are very soft and mushy.

2 Adjust the seasoning if necessary, adding a little more lemon juice for a tangier flavour, if liked. Transfer to a bowl and serve warm or cold.

MULLED CRANBERRY & RED WINE

750 ml (1¼ pint) bottle
   inexpensive red wine
600 ml (1 pint) cranberry juice
100 ml (3½ fl oz) brandy, rum,
   vodka or orange liqueur
100 g (3½ oz) caster sugar
1 orange
8 cloves
1–2 cinnamon sticks (depending
   on size)

To serve
1 orange, cut into segments
2–3 bay leaves
few fresh cranberries

Makes **8–10 glasses**
Prep time **10 minutes**
Cooking time **10 minutes**

1 Pour the red wine, cranberry juice and brandy or other alcohol into a large saucepan and stir in the sugar.

2 Stud the orange segments with a clove. Break the cinnamon sticks into large pieces and add to the pan with the orange pieces. Cover with a lid and heat gently for about 10 minutes until warm.

3 Replace the orange segments with fresh ones and add the bay leaves and cranberries. Ladle into heatproof glasses or mugs, keeping back the fruits and herbs, if liked.

Frothy Hot Toddy
CHOCOLATE DRINK

1 teaspoon cornflour
300 ml (½ pint) semi-skimmed milk
1 teaspoon golden granulated sugar
4 squares of plain dark chocolate
2 tablespoons alcohol of your choice (such as brandy, rum or vodka)
1 teaspoon chocolate (plain dark, milk or white), grated, to serve

Serves **1**
Prep time **5 minutes**
Cooking time **5 minutes**

1 Put the cornflour in a jug and mix in 1 tablespoon of the milk to make a smooth paste. Stir in 200 ml (7 fl oz) of the milk, the sugar, chocolate and alcohol.

2 Pour into a saucepan and heat through until hot, then pour into a tall mug.

3 Heat the remaining milk and whisk vigorously. Pour over the hot chocolate, sprinkle over the grated chocolate and serve immediately.

RUSTY NAIL

AN AFTER-DINNER DRINK THE NAME OF WHICH
IS PROBABLY BECAUSE OF ITS COLOUR RATHER THAN
IMMIGRANT SCOTTISH BARTENDERS STIRRING THE
COCKTAIL WITH A RUSTY NAIL BEFORE SERVING IT
TO THEIR AMERICAN PATRONS, AS LEGEND HAS IT.

ice cubes, if available
1½ measures Scotch whisky
1 measure Drambuie

Serves 1
Prep time **3 minutes**

1 Fill a short glass with ice cubes, if using. Pour over the
whisky and Drambuie and serve.

Whisky MAC

A WARMING SLUG MADE WITH EQUAL MEASURES OF SCOTCH AND GINGER WINE,
THIS IS A DELICIOUS PICK-ME-UP.

3-4 ice cubes, if available
1 measure Scotch whisky
1 measure ginger wine

Serves 1
Prep time **3 minutes**

1 Put the ice cubes, if using, in a short glass. Pour over the
whisky and ginger wine, stir lightly and serve.

Pimm's Cocktail

1   Fill a tall glass with ice, if using, then add the Pimm's.

2   Put the cucumber and fruit slices in the glass and top up with the lemonade. Decorate with the mint sprig and serve.

ice cubes, if available
1 measure Pimm's No. 1
cucumber slices
1 strawberry
apple slices
lemon slices
orange slices
3 measures lemonade
1 mint sprig, to garnish

Serves 1
Prep time 10 minutes

INDEX

ACKNOWLEDGEMENTS

Picture Credits
Key: a above, b below, c center, l left, r right, bk background

CGTextures 32 bk (throughout), 47 bk (throughout), 149 bk (throughout), 163 bk; Jacobo Cortés Ferreira 20 bk (throughout). Octopus Publishing Group 25, 251; Craig Robertson; 12 br, 26; David Jordan 15; David Loftus 201; David Munns 181, 249; Gareth Sambridge 237; Ian Garlick 179 ar, 205; Ian Wallace 2 a, 12 al, 12 ar, 19, 27, 39 al, 39 b, 40, 43, 48, 49, 61, 68, 71, 73, 75, 77, 89, 93 c, 96, 122, 144, 152, 155, 165, 187, 226 ar, 230, 242; Lis Parsons 2 b, 2 c, 12 bl, 16, 21, 39 ar, 41, 55, 56, 57, 65, 72, 78, 85, 93 a, 95, 99, 105, 106, 107, 111, 143, 146 bl, 149, 161, 168, 169, 173, 175, 179 b, 184, 189, 191, 197, 226 al, 226 bl, 235, 238, 240, 241, 245; Sean Myers 228; Simon Smith 133, 137; Stephen Conroy 13, 33, 37, 51, 69, 81, 93 b, 101, 118, 119, 127, 128, 135, 146 al, 146 ar, 151, 153, 157, 179 al, 183, 193, 194, 217 b, 219, 220, 222, 224, 226, 236, 247; William Reavell 139, 167, 209, 213; William Shaw 53, 121, 126, 130, 136, 146 br, 158, 162, 177, 185, 195, 239. Shutterstock Anastasiia Sorokina 4 a; Andrew Helbig 6 a; Andrey_Kuzmin 178-179 bk; aodaodaodaod 2-3 bk (throughout); artfood 146-147 bk; bikeriderlondon 115 a; BrAt82 12-13 bk (throughout), 15 bk (throughout); CandyBox Images 114; cobraphotography 216; Cranach 43 bk (throughout); Dutourdumonde Photography 5 b; Dzinnik Darius 217 a; Fedorov Oleksiy 23 bk (throughout); Goodluz 115 b; Grischa Georgiew 5 a; Jason Patrick Ross 83 a; kao 1 bk (throughout); Kotenko Oleksandr 83 b; lightpoet 82; Loskutnikov 18 bk (throughout); magicinfoto 8 bk (throughout); mama_mia 29 l; mapraest 6 br; margouillat photo 125; Naffarts 6 bl; narinto 28-29 bk (throughout); Sander van der Werf 9; Svetlana Lukienko 28; Tanya Lomakivska 170; Triff 31 bk (throughout). Thinkstock donstock 29 b; EnginKorkmaz 6-7 bk (throughout); 60 bk (throughout); Fuse 171 b; loops7 14 bk (throughout); Madredus 30 bk (throughout); MKucova 171 a; ongap 3; Steve Mason 29 r; Oksana Lebedev 4-5 bk (throughout).

Publisher Sarah Ford
Editor Pauline Bache
Features Writer Cara Frost-Sharratt
Designers Eoghan O'Brien and Jaz Bahra
Picture Library Manager Jennifer Veall
Assistant Production Manager Lucy Carter